Addison Mizner
Architect of Dreams and R
(1872-1933)

AN EXHIBITION ORGANIZED BY THE NORTON GALLERY OF ART

Text by Christina Orr

NORTON GALLERY OF ART
SOCIETY OF THE FOUR ARTS
THE HENRY MORRISON FLAGLER MUSEUM
and The Historical Society of Palm Beach County
MARCH 5 - APRIL 17, 1977

Library of Congress Cataloging in Publication Data
Main entry under title:

Addison Mizner (1872-1933)
Architect of Dreams and Realities.

Includes bibliographical references.
1. Mizner, Addison, 1872-1933. I. Orr, Christina,
1947-   . II. Norton Gallery and School of Art,
Palm Beach, Fla.
NA737.M59A64   720.92'4   77-858

This exhibition was organized with the aid of a grant from the National Endowment for the Arts in Washington, D.C., a Federal agency.

This project was made possible in part through a grant from the Fine Arts Council of Florida, an agency within the Division of Cultural Affairs, the Department of State, and the National Endowment for the Arts, a Federal agency.

Permission to reprint any of the information presented in this catalogue must be received from the author.
All photography credits are given in parentheses following captions. Permission to reprint copyrighted Kuhner photographs must be received from the artist.

M Acknowledgements

With much appreciation I thank the following people for their supreme effort on behalf of this exhibition: Miss Alice DeLamar, Mr. and Mrs. Lester Geisler, Mr. and Mrs. Kim Hollins, Mrs. Landes Lewitin, Mr. Karl Riddle, Mrs. H. H. Smith, Mr. Alex Waugh, Mr. and Mrs. Marion Sims Wyeth. Miss Alice DeLamar should be singled out for her enthusiasm and encouragement at all stages — adversities and advances alike.

Much assistance and information was received from the following people who were associates, employees, or friends of Addison Mizner: Mr. Draper Babcock, Mr. Rankin Bingham, Justice E. Harris Drew, Mr. José Diaz, Mr. Carl LeVander, Miss Anita Loos, Mr. Joe Mueller, Mr. Herman Reich, Mr. F. L. Schindler, Mrs. Byron Simonson, Mr. Bror Tingstrom, Mr. John Volk, Mr. Arie Veldhuizen, Mr. George Votaw, Mrs. Ruth Winslow.

Thanks are also extended to the following groups which represent only a portion of those which were involved in the research: Boynton Woman's Club, Boca Raton Historical Society, Boca Raton Cloisters, California Historical Society, Department of Architecture at the University of Miami, The Everglades Club, Gulf Stream Golf Club, Palm Beach Daily News, Riverside Baptist Church, Sea Island Club, Society for the Preservation of Long Island Antiquities, and the Solano County (California) Historical Society.

Special acknowledgment should be given to the Directors of the three museums involved in the exhibition: Mr. Richard Madigan of the Norton Gallery of Art, Mr. John Gordon of the Society of the Four Arts, and Mr. Charles Simmons of The Henry Morrison Flagler Museum. The efforts of The Historical Society of Palm Beach County and its Directors were most appreciated. The staffs of all of the institutions involved deserve much congratulation. The entire staff of the Norton Gallery participated in this exhibition. Jayne Horrocks, my secretary, managed to keep me organized and for that she should receive a medal. The maintenance staff under the guidance of Phelps Merrell tackled what seemed to be an impossibly complex installation. Sue Whitman, in charge of public relations, reached out nationally and achieved her goal. Addison thanks you. At the other institutions I must, from my own experience, single out Mrs. Helen McKinney and Mrs. Evelyn Rand of the Society of the Four Arts Library; Ms. Cathryn J. McElroy and Ms. Merri Ferrell of The Henry Morrison Flagler Museum, and Mrs. Maxine Banash of The Historical Society of Palm Beach County.

Craig Kuhner, the architectural photographer, worked long, hard, and diligently. His intense dedication is obvious in his work. The entire installation was designed and coordinated by Elizabeth Plater-Zyberk, a Miami-based architect. Her creativity and perseverance combined to create a fine exhibition. Mr. Jim Baker of Southeastern Printing designed the catalogue, a publication sensitive to the architecture of Addison Mizner.

Robert Orr continually reconvinced me to keep tackling this project. June Neubauer was a fine friend who knew how to change the subject. Richard Cahall listened to my complaints, patted my head, and pushed me forward — sometimes simultaneously. Wolsey Orr absorbed a few tears, but seems none the worse for wear.

The lenders and those who permitted us to photograph their Mizner buildings were essential to the success of this undertaking. And last, but certainly not least, I must thank the National Endowment for the Arts and the Fine Arts Council of Florida without whose financial support this exhibition would have been impossible.

Christina Orr
Curator, Norton Gallery of Art

Addison Mizner on the building site of the Woman's Club, Boynton, 1925. (Ray Dame)

⋀ Foreward

This catalogue and exhibition are the first presentation of Addison Mizner's architecture and decorative arts since the 1928 publication of Ida M. Tarbell's *Florida Architecture of Addison Mizner*.[1] In the 1920's Mizner was, without exaggeration, the best-known and most-discussed living American architect. He was emulated by many architects, an emulation which continues in Florida to the present. He was employed by the privileged few for Mizner was a "social" architect whose greatest testaments are mansions and private clubs.

Addison Mizner was an architect with a philosophy and a dream. Personally, he was an intelligent, articulate, and extremely well-read, kind, sensitive man. He was a man with a great sense of humor — of outspoken wit. It is this last quality which many people remember foremost and unfortunately often to the detriment of his architecture and decorative arts. Mizner could joke with and about his clients. He was honest and courageous enough to admit, "If an architect could chloroform his client, the house would be more attractive and coherent."[2] But, as a designer he was not the buffoon which Palm Beach folklore presents. It has become an accepted fact that Mizner forgot kitchens, baths, staircases, and any and all other essentials while remembering to include "forty car garages" in his buildings. This is absurdity. It was time that an accurate and comprehensive look be given the public so that you could appraise Mizner, his achievements, and his abilities for yourselves. In a 1928 review of Tarbell's *Florida Architecture of Addison Mizner*, the critic of the *International Studio*, which was a journal associated with the highly esteemed *Connoisseur*, wrote:

Every once in a while in the course of the world's development some architect gets a supremely good chance to impress his personality upon his local background. That happened when Pericles passed over the adornment of the Acropolis to his personal architect, and when the Renaissance Popes entrusted the new St. Peter's to Bramante and Michelangelo. And, if the comparison be thought not too topheavy, a similar occasion was offered by Palm Beach to Addison Mizner. Against the at times tawdry and gingerbread meretriciousness of the pre-Mizner Palm Beach background the solidity and opulence of the Mizner architecture scheme stands out with a definiteness which, to an almost justifiable degree, is comparable with that of the Acropolis and St. Peter's against their background.[3]

Even this author, who is a great admirer of the architecture of Addison Mizner, believes that the *Studio* critic overstated his case, but the point should be well-taken that Mizner's contemporaries held him in the highest regard. Fifty years of verbal history have tarnished Mizner's image, while the buildings which should reflect his quality as an architect are overlooked. Via Mizner and Via Parigi exist today almost as they did a half century ago — as popular as ever. Not one Mizner building has been demolished for structural reasons. Mizner homes have retained their elegance and their functionalism. This three-part exhibition is an effort to set the record straight.

The Henry Morrison Flagler Museum and The Historical Society of Palm Beach County are presenting Mizner's memorabilia and objects relating to his years in Guatemala, Alaska, and other exotic ports of call. They also have the portion of the exhibition which is devoted to architectural preservation. Numerous Mizner buildings have been demolished, including the three most monumental Mizner houses ("El Mirasol" for Edward T. Stotesbury, "Playa Riente" for Joshua S. Cosden, and "Casa Bendita" for John S. Phipps). Other buildings have been vastly altered; some even physically divided into separate buildings. Still others are threatened with destruction. It is essential for the cultural heritage of Palm Beach and the United States that the Mizner buildings not only be saved from demolition but also from severe disfiguration.

The Norton Gallery of Art and the Society of the Four Arts both offer watercolor sketches, architectural drawings, design scrapbooks, furniture, pottery, stonework, ironwork, and glass designed by Mizner and his capable office and by the Mizner Industries staff. The Norton Gallery of Art will concentrate on the earlier periods of Mizner's career from San Francisco in the 1890's to New York City and Long Island in the 1900's through Palm Beach in 1924. The Boca Raton and Singer's Island projects will be the concentration at the Society of the Four Arts, which itself was designed by Mizner as The Embassy Club in 1928-29. The later Florida and California houses and projects for nationally-scattered locations will also be shown. The Norton Gallery of Art will display the Addison Mizner Crucifix Collection which is a part of that museum's permanent holdings. This rare collection was recently reevaluated by Dr. Walter Cahn, an outstanding Medieval art historian at Yale University. Contemporary photographs of Mizner's work by Craig Kuhner, an architectural photographer on the faculty of Ball State University in Indiana, will be exhibited at all three museums.

It is suggested that the exhibition be visited in chronological order: The Henry Morrison Flagler Museum, the Norton Gallery of Art, the Society of the Four Arts.

The catalogue is also divided chronologically for the convenience of the museum visitor. The emphasis is on the architecture of Addison Mizner with a last section devoted to the decorative arts products of Mizner Industries. The text is illustrated with early photographs, sketches, architectural drawings (plans, elevations, details), and contemporary photographs. A checklist of buildings and projects is included at the end of the catalogue. It was considered more important to explain Mizner's experiences, architectural philosophy, and his design process than to consume precious space with descriptive discussions of individual buildings and with an object checklist.

As the author of this catalogue and the creator of this exhibition, I am the first to acknowledge that errors will be made. I extend my apologies and I will appreciate informed, documented corrections. This project is an outgrowth of three years of doctoral dissertation research at Yale University. No material published on Addison Mizner after his death in 1933 could be considered accurate as mythology quickly mixed with fact. Virtually no research had been conducted on Mizner's pre-Palm Beach career and it was with great difficulty and extensive travel that the activities of those years came to light. Research on the Long Island period is still continuing. The sources used included unpublished Mizner manuscripts and papers, original Mizner sketchbooks, scrapbooks and architectural drawings, and verbal or written interviews with remaining architectural and decorative arts associates, friends, and family. Research was conducted in New Haven, New York City, Washington, D.C., many cities of Florida, California, Long Island, Guatemala, and Spain. A carefully selected bibliography of accurate sources on Mizner's architecture and decorative arts is included in this publication.

It is our hope that the general public will learn from this exhibition. It is time that the shop-worn Mizner stories disappear and that Floridians, in particular, be proud of their adopted son and understand his place in American architecture. However, above all, it is hoped that the general public will enjoy this exhibition for public enjoyment was a primary goal of Mizner's architecture.

Christina Orr

1 Ida M. Tarbell, *Florida Architecture of Addison Mizner*, William Helburn, Inc., New York City, 1928.

2 "The Florida House", an interview of Addison Mizner by John Taylor Boyd in *Arts and Decoration*, January, 1930, Vol. 32, p. 37.

3 "Addison Mizner and Florida", a review by Curtis Patterson, *International Studio*, 1928, Vol. 90, p. 72.

Born in Benicia, California in 1872 to a fine, established family, Addison Cairns Mizner had no reason to believe that he could not pursue his whims and moods, as long as he maintained the respect of the mother he adored. His father, Lansing Bond Mizner, was a successful landowner, lawyer, and politician who had run for the Governorship of the new state to lose by only a narrow margin. Older brothers, Lansing, Edgar, William, and Henry had entered respectable professions, while sister Min had married to advantage. Addison from early childhood had been inclined towards the arts and specifically towards architecture, but the family frowned upon his goals. Only with half-humor Addison wrote, "When William took his first trip to China [ca. 1893-94] as ship's doctor, I was sent along to prevent me becoming an artist, which the family said was the lowest form of long-haired, flowing-cravat ass extant."[1] Yes, Addison was outspoken, a good trait which at times caused consternation among friends and provided fertile breeding grounds for stories and myths. Another of Addison's traits was to do what he thought best and also to work hard to achieve his goals. Addison made the decision to become an architect, and he became a fine one, the best-known American architect of the frenzied, fabulous decade of the 1920's.

To retrace a bit, it should be realized that Addison's childhood was a cosmopolitan experience. Benicia on the northern part of San Francisco Bay was the capital of California. Statesmen, writers, and myriads of other interesting, influential people passed through the Mizner home, a rambling prefabricated house which had been transported around the Cape. Trips to nearby San Francisco were frequent. Childhood was, however, childhood and Addison along with his younger brother Wilson (b. 1876) were terrors. In 1888 while "jumping over the fire" on the 4th of July, Addison fell and injured his leg, a problem which plagued him throughout the remainder of his life. In 1889, "Papa" Mizner was appointed "minister", ambassador, to the five republics of Latin America, an area presently encompassing Guatemala, San Salvador, Nicaragua, Costa Rica, and Panama. The position was an important one as negotiations for a cross-continental canal were embryonic. In describing his arrival by ship at the Mexican port of Mazatlan on the trip south to Guatemala, Addison wrote, "It probably was the greatest day of my life, for there lying white in the sun was my first Spanish town."[2] From that moment Mizner was captivated by Spanish architecture and the remainder of his life, with a few moments taken out for fun, was dedicated to understanding the essence of Spanish sixteenth and seventeenth century architectural design; reinterpreting, synthesizing, and updating its aesthetic principles. The impact that Guatemala had upon the impressionable, romantic Addison can probably not be overstated. Remembering some forty years later Mizner wrote:

An hour or two later we boarded the train again, and began to climb the mountains. Little by little the growth changed. Chattering monkeys gave way to squirrels, and squawking parrots and macaws to mocking birds. Nothing I have ever seen is more astonishingly beautiful than that trip [San José de Guatemala to Guatemala City]. We climbed over five thousand feet, and just before sunset got our first glimpse of Guatemala City, lying like an opal, with its great expanse of colored houses and churches.[3]

Studying at the Instituto Nacional, Mizner became fluent in Spanish, an essential tool which he used throughout his architectural career. He came to know the Hispanic people and he began to understand the Spanish culture. Although convalescing from his leg injury, Mizner was able to visit many different places in all five countries, but he had to remain relatively inactive so he spent much of his time sketching with watercolors which had just been presented to him on the trip south.

Addison Mizner with his family in Benicia, California, ca. 1884. (left to right) *Lansing Bond Mizner* (extreme left, beard); *Ella Watson Mizner,* , his wife (with her hand on his shoulder), and seven of their eight children: *Edgar* (top); *Lansing* (derby) and *William* (fob); *Wilson* (in front of his mother); *Minnie*; *Henry* (straw hat); *Addison* (seated in front of Wilson, wearing a tam); in the garden of their Benicia home.

Returning to San Francisco in ca. the fall of 1890 to attend school at Bates in San Rafael and Boones in Berkeley, the peripatetic portion of Mizner's life begins. His experiences were far too varied to be discussed fully in this catalogue. Mizner prepared for the examinations at the University of California at Berkeley, but "having had no foundation to build an education on,"[4] he failed. He lived briefly at the Occidental Hotel in San Francisco with his parents, who had left Guatemala when Papa Mizner became seriously ill, until his parents moved to Honolulu in the hope of improving his father's health.

Addison, at twenty, was to remain in San Francisco and look after Wilson, sixteen and inscrutable. Perhaps the task was insurmountable for in 1892-93 Addison studied at the University of Salamanca in Salamanca, Spain.[5] In the late nineteenth century aspiring artists and architects often matriculated at European universities without any intentions of receiving degrees, which were then still considered unnecessary in the United States. American architecture schools were new phenomena and were principally geared to mechanical drawing and engineering rather than to architectural history and design. Most Americans attended the Ecole des Beaux Arts in Paris, but others chose to study in London, Berlin, Italy or Spain. Mizner presumably went to Salamanca because of his interest in Spanish architecture, his fluency in the Spanish language, and the potential benefits from family connections. At the University Mizner would have attended courses in the division of humanities, receiving a heavy dose of Spanish history, literature, and philosophy. No architecture per se was taught, but in Spanish humanities education, art and architecture have always played prominent roles.[6] From his later architecture, design scrapbooks, and writings, it is apparent that Mizner was fond of Salamanca, well-versed in its simple golden-stoned architecture, and influenced in his own design by the city.

For his "practical" training Mizner returned to San Francisco and "...went in to Willis Polk, who was a young architect of great taste and little work, and applied as an apprentice draftsman."[7] Willis Polk, in 1894 a young and innovative architect, was later to become a key figure in San Francisco design, an active and influential participant in the reconstruction of the city after the 1906 earthquake, and a principal proponent of the Spanish "Mission" style.[8]

By piecing together bits of information from Mizner and Polk material with addresses in the *Directory to San Francisco*,[9] it appears that Addison worked with Polk in 1894, 1895, and possibly in 1896. In a Mizner design scrapbook there is a drawing in Mizner's distinct rendering style for a half-timbered house. On the back is the red stamp "This drawing must be returned to Polk and Polk Architects, Room 1, Tenth Floor, Mills Building".[10] The Polk firm was only located in the Mills Building in 1894.

Since the Polk firm did have limited work and was never larger than Willis, his brother, his father, Addison, and Wilson Mizner, who was described as an "artist" for the firm but who apparently did nothing, it is not illogical to assume that the four architects all played a part in designing, although Addison's primary duty must have been drafting. It is certain that Addison considered himself an architect for in the city directory of 1895 he placed the following listing, "Mizner, Addison C., Architect, r[esidence] 1520 Clay". And the point which must be made is that the rest of the world considered Mizner an architect. For turn-of-the-century people Mizner had completed all the requirements necessary to be an architect and in fact his credentials would have been considered quite prestigious. No degrees were required. No examinations were given. No licenses were issued. Demanded was a thorough knowledge of architectural history and practical training in drafting. Whatever buildings Mizner may have designed and drafted with Willis Polk remain unidentified, largely in part to the loss of archival ma-

Half-timbered House, pencil drawing with colored crayon highlights, ca. 1894 from Addison Mizner's scrapbook, "English Gothic". (Lee Brian)

terials and actual buildings in the fires of the 1906 earthquake.

Mizner did move in with Willis Polk to a strange house on Russian Hill, probably in the fall of 1895 for Mizner described working on *The Lark*, a journal published by Polk and his friends from June, 1895 to April, 1897. Mizner commented, "*The Lark*, a monthly pamphlet, was written on our dining room table. Gelet (sic) Burgess, Willis Polk, and others, subscribing, while I acted as sub-editor."[11] It was at this time that Mizner was made a partner in the firm, a dubious financial achievement but a firm stepping-stone. Mizner remarked, "My salary was microscopic, and half the time unpaid. So Willis took me in as a partner, and I got first one and then another good job."[12]

The experience of working with Willis Polk must have been a most positive one for Mizner. He mingled with the young intelligentsia and was a part, although to what degree it is no longer known, of the avant-garde movement, architectural, artistic, and literary of the 1890's in San Francisco. It was a provocative learning experience, exactly the non-academic impetus that Addison needed. He wrote:

I was working hard and took architecture very seriously. Willis had a good, although small, library; and wherein I had not been a worker at school, I became an absorbed student. Even through later frivolities, I put in a specified amount of labor at the drawing board, and at all odd moments you could find me with a book in my hand. Strange to say, I liked good things and mentally had plenty of 'whys' and 'whens?' When was the chimney place invented, or what did the barber pole represent; all intrigued me immensely.[13]

The Lark was a delicate combination of spoof, cynicism, and avant-gardism. Addison must have been in his glory. Although the publication was relatively short-lived, it did receive national attention. A Milwaukee paper commented,

"A whimsical but ingenious little magazine—the strangest pronouncement yet of the fin-de-siecle spirit of artistic revolt against the commonplace. There is nothing quite like it." And the refined *New York Times* printed, "The writers of THE LARK appear to have taken seriously the title of 'Les Jeunes', which the *Times* conferred upon them last May. What we intended to say was 'les Jaunes', apropos of their Chinese paper. But surely *L'Arkitecture Moderne* justifies the former spelling."[14]

In November 1897, Edgar, who was with the Alaska Commercial Company, Addison, William and Wilson all headed north to the Alaskan gold fields in an effort to "strike it rich". They were still young and adventurous, and inspired by the family's dismal financial situation which had been a result of the death of Papa Mizner on Addison's twenty-first birthday. Addison returned from the gold fields in 1899 with a sizeable "purse" which he invested wisely for he had faced the prospect of poverty and did not care to repeat the experience. Addison was an honest, diligent man who loved the good life but who accepted the responsibility of supporting himself after his father's death.[15]

After altering a honeymoon cottage for an old friend, Andrew Martin, in Palm Springs,[16] Mizner attempted to resurrect his architectural career. In ca. 1899 he moved to Honolulu with the promise of a major architectural commission. The project never materialized and Mizner instead painted miniature ivories, sketched portraits, wrote the first of the *Cynics' Calendars* with Ethel Watts Mumford, assisted in taking panoramic photographs of the Islands, and eventually moved on to Apia, Samoa, and another round of new experiences.

In 1904 Mizner recognized that "...working as a draftsman didn't seem to be getting me anywhere and every successful architect was a doddering old man".[17] He decided to return to Guatemala, supposedly to negotiate lucrative coffee contracts. Once again Guatemala captured Mizner's romantic mind and he reimmersed himself in Spanish Colonial architecture. The country was in a state of political, economic, and religious upheaval. Catholicism was all but defunct with churches and monasteries in abandon more often than in operation. Mizner, loving the Spanish Colonial artifacts, purchased them with the prospect of resale in the United States. Spanish had become quite the vogue in New York and priceless Guatemalan church vestments, silver, choir stalls, and all other religious accouterments were being pilfered by the natives or left to rot in the natural elements. Exportation was preservation as well as profit. Mizner carefully and correctly explained his actions, "I mean no disrespect to the church, and it should be understood that it was legitimate at this time for the priests to sell, and that they were near starvation."[18] There is no doubt that Mizner bought in quantity with the idea of resale, but he was only participating in what was an acceptable trade for Americans until well after the second World War. Perhaps the description of an old monastery Mizner purchased will enlighten the reader as to his intent and vision. He wrote, "The reason I wanted it was that eight of the side chapels of the church were intact and in each stood, thirty feet high, carved wood altars with heavy gilding. I could see in my mind's eye a beautiful panelled room made from them."[19]

The majority of Mizner's time was spent in Antigua, Guatemala, a magnificent town which had been the capital until earthquakes forced its abandonment. Antigua contained gems of buildings from the sixteenth and seventeenth centuries. Since it had been a governmental, educational, commercial, and religious center, Antigua had all types of buildings, including outstanding examples of residential architecture.[20] Having known the town in 1889, Mizner diligently explored it as an adult and as an architect. His small sketchbooks contain numerous pen and ink over pencil and simple pencil sketches of major Antiguan monuments and of architectural details which attracted him. As indicated by his

View of the Church of the La Merced, Antigua, Guatemala, Sept. 24th, 1904, ink over pencil sketch from Mizner's scrapbook, "Spain and its Colonies". (Lee Brian)

Wooden Window Grille, Antigua, Guatemala, Sept. 20th, 1904, ink over pencil sketch from Mizner's scrapbook, "Spain and its Colonies". (Lee Brian)

drawings, he was enthusiastic about the Church of the La Merced, a reconstructed sixteenth and seventeenth century structure. He studied its ribbed dome, its ornate entrance facade, its majestic fountain which occupies almost the whole of a grand interior courtyard. There are also pen and ink sketches of Antigua's central fountain with bare-breasted women spewing forth water, of complicated wooden window grilles, of corner window details, of carved mermaids flanking a doorway—of similar architectural details which captured Mizner's interest.[21] The sketches seem somewhat forced and constricted, lacking the freedom of Mizner's watercolor drawings. But, they are studies of existing architecture, drawn for the sheer understanding of spatial relationships, for the comprehension of intricate detail, and above all as an aid to memory.

Although numerically older, Mizner nonetheless retained some of his youthful romantic feelings for Guatemala. He was still enchanted by the play of strong Guatemalan light on austere buildings. The foil for a building was an integral part of the architecture. In Mizner's description of Antigua's central plaza, the blend of architect and romantic is obvious:

On one side of the enormous plaza the arcades of the vice-regal palace run the whole length; at the far end the arcades of private palaces; and nearest us are those of the barracks; all in good order and in use; across the end stands the front of the old cathedral, with only part of it in use, for the back is a huge ruin, although over 30 of its flat domes form a terrace to which we climb to see the sunset.[22]

1 Addison Mizner, *The Many Mizners*, Sears Publishing Co., New York City, 1932, pp. 64-65. Much information, substantiated by further research, was found in this highly accurate autobiography.

2 *Ibid.*, p. 45.

3 *Ibid.*, p. 47.

4 *Ibid.*, p. 63.

5 Records at the University of Salamanca do not list foreign students unless they received degrees. All of Mizner's associates and friends did not doubt that Mizner attended the University. The *Palm Beach Social Directory* of 1925 listed under the entry for Addison Mizner, "College — Salmonica (sic) '94", Vol. 1, p. 77.

6 For the curriculum and historical information consult Julian Alvarez Villar, *La Universidad de Salamanca*, Universidad de Salamanca, 1973.

7 *The Many Mizners*, p. 64.

8 Richard W. Longstreth, a scholar who is preparing his doctoral dissertation for the University of California at Berkeley on Willis Polk, aided in this portion of the Mizner research. He also remains uncertain of Mizner's role in and years with the firm. The Polk archives are scanty for the early period.

9 *Polk's (Langley's) Directory to San Francisco*, San Francisco, individual volumes for 1890-1898. The author of this directory is no relation to the architect. Individual entries for Willis Polk, Polk and Polk, and all Mizners were researched.

10 Addison Mizner scrapbook, "English Gothic", Mizner Collection at the Society of the Four Arts Library, Palm Beach, Florida.

11 *The Many Mizners*, p. 75. Mizner admitted to being a poor speller and he must have been closely watched as a sub-editor.

12 *Ibid.*, pp. 74-75.

13 *Ibid.*, p. 74.

14 These comments appeared on the flyleaf of *The Lark*, San Francisco, February, 1896, No. 10. It was assumed that they were genuine, since the publication was well-known in literary circles.

15 Information on Alaska was obtained from Mizner's photoalbums in the collection of the Mizner family.

16 This house remains unlocated.

17 *The Many Mizners*, p. 217.

18 *Ibid.*, p. 223.

19 *Ibid.*, p. 224.

20 J. Joaquin Pardo, Pedro Zamora Castellanos, Luis Lujan Muñoz, *Guía de Antigua Guatemala*, José de Pineda Ibarra, Guatemala, 3rd ed., 1969.

21 Addison Mizner sketchbook, no title, dated Guatemala, 1904 in the collection of the Mizner family. Also drawings can be found in the Mizner scrapbooks, "Spain and its Colonies" and "Spain and its Colonies II", Mizner Collection at the Society of the Four Arts Library, Palm Beach, Florida.

22 *The Many Mizners*, p. 223.

New York was the glittering city—a place difficult to brave but essential to confront—the social, cultural, architectural center of the United States. In the fall of 1904 Mizner took an apartment in the Old Livingstone House at 24th Street and began to sell his Guatemalan treasures. Assured of an income from these sales and his old Klondike investment, he felt able to "...struggle with architecture again".[1]

Between 1905 and 1908 Mizner traveled extensively, concentrating on his architectural interests. He began putting together scrapbooks dedicated to "Architecture of the United States", "Furniture", "Greece, Rome, Italy", "England", "France", and "Egypt and the Far East" in which he placed photographs, postcards, and clippings of buildings and of architectural details which interested him.[2] He also pasted in his own drawings, often merely quick sketches on scraps of paper. Frequently, measurements, color notes, and descriptions in Mizner's hand attend these scrapbook illustrations. In later years these books were used as inspiration for designs, as indicated by Mizner's remark, "We left Paris [for Italy] a couple of weeks later [winter, 1905] and I spent half of my time in shops buying photographs of palaces and cathedrals, that I wasn't to use for many years, as I only got bungalows and warehouses to build at first."[3]

Another 1905 turning-point for Mizner was his introduction to Stanford White of McKim, Mead, and White, the great architectural firm responsible for many of the Newport, Rhode Island mansions. It must have been a momentous occasion for Mizner to meet the great "social" architect as his scrapbook, "Architecture of the United States", is laden with clippings of buildings by White. Mizner must have admired the flatness of White's later buildings, the historical orthodoxy of his designs, his masterful control of scale, and his perfect synthesis of detail with facade.[4] In one scrapbook there is a measured sketch for a fireplace, drawn on the back of Lamb's Club stationery, with a note in Mizner's hand, "Old Italian mantel presented to the Lamb's Club by Stan-

ford White."[5] A second roughly-sketched drawing of a baroque ceiling bears the following Mizner notations, "Quarter section in House of Stanford White Dining Room 1905" and near an acanthus leaf, "gilt inside turnover dull black...almost every Miler (?) leaf is at a different angle and the ribbons are in the middle of every panel...stock acanthus gilt on dirty white/Indian red...garland of oak or laurel with fruit embossed ribons (sic) and stems gilt fruit-old red pink-leaves chocotale (sic)."[6] It may even be that Mizner was finishing this ceiling for Stanford White who was apparently turning over jobs, particularly the refurbishment of brownstones and the interior decoration of houses, too small for his prestigious firm to Mizner.[7]

Mizner's admiration for Stanford White cannot be overstressed and it is unfortunate that more cannot be discovered about the friendship. Years after achieving success Mizner wrote in his autobiography, "I got to know Mr. White

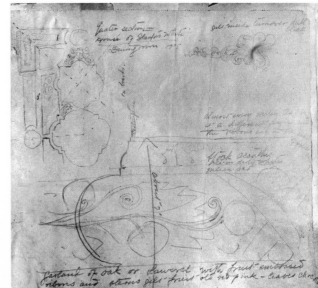

"Quarter section in House of Stanford White Dining Room 1905", pencil sketch with Mizner's notations from scrapbook, "Greece, Rome, Italy". (Lee Brian)

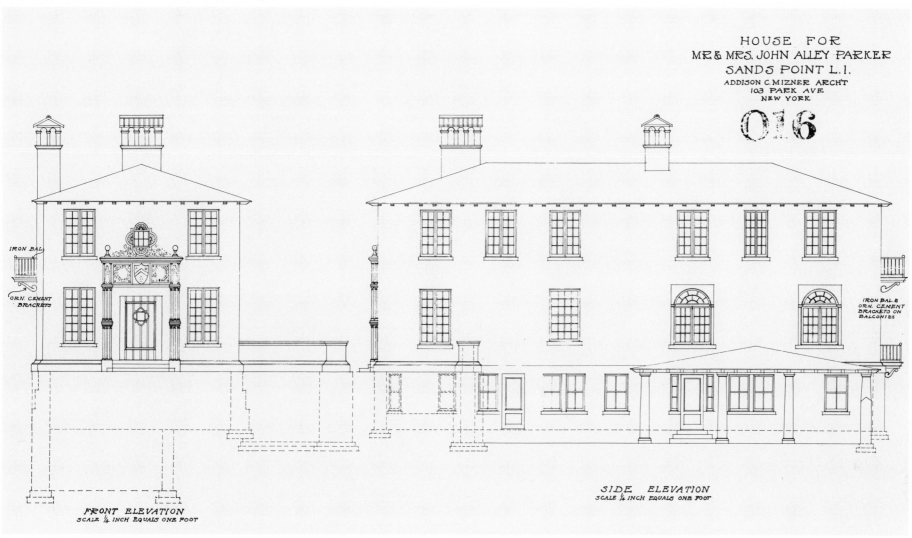

HOUSE FOR
MR & MRS. JOHN ALLEY PARKER
SANDS POINT L.I.
ADDISON C. MIZNER ARCH'T
103 PARK AVE
NEW YORK
016

IRON BAL.

ORN. CEMENT
BRACKETS

IRON BAL. &
ORN. CEMENT
BRACKETS ON
BALCONIES

FRONT ELEVATION
SCALE ¼ INCH EQUALS ONE FOOT

SIDE ELEVATION
SCALE ¼ INCH EQUALS ONE FOOT

Front and Side Elevations of a House for Mr. and Mrs. John Alley Parker, Sands Point, L.I., 1912. Ink on glossy linen.

very well and as I was not pushing for jobs, he used to like to sit and talk architecture to someone who knew so little about it. I worshipped him, for he was my God."[8]

By 1908 Mizner was listed in *Trow's General Directory of New York City* as "Mizner, Edison (sic) architect h[ouse] 22 W. 8th St."[9] Mizner considered his first significant com-

mission to have been the completion and interior decoration of a townhouse at 154 E. 70th Street for Mrs. Stephen Brown, who had hired Mizner after becoming disenchanted with her architect midstream in the construction of her house in 1912.[10] The house was a Collegiate Gothic design, well-proportioned and admirably detailed but exceedingly flat.

In claiming this as his first major achievement, Mizner did himself some disservice, although it may have been the first commission for the social set who were to be his main patrons. In 1907 he had supervised the refurbishment of the Hotel Rand, also known as the Mizner and Barnes Hotel, at 142 W. 49th Street.[11] In 1910 Mizner had restored and altered a Colonial clapboard house, The Old Cow Bay Manor House, at Whitestone Landing near Port Washington, Long Island for his own residence. An early article on the house in *Architectural Record* is most revealing for although Mizner made alterations to the building he had respect for its historical place in American architectural design. The original portion of the house dated from 1673 with additions in 1795, 1812, and in 1910 by Mizner who did not touch the old portions of the house, retaining its neo-classical front door, its wainscotted dining room, and its formal stair set in a narrow hall. He added a kitchen and a pantry and extended the front porch to three times its original width while keeping the old columns and their capitals in a portico effect.[12]

Among Mizner's known architectural commissions, and there are countless which will never be known in this period, is a residence for Mr. and Mrs. John Alley Parker of Sands Point, Long Island. The extant drawings for that house bear the following stamp, "Addison Mizner Arch. 103 Park Ave., New York" and are dated in January and September, 1912.[13] The residence has details which anticipate Mizner's later style. The main facade has an ornate quasi-Spanish doorway and the roof, although not of red tile, had Spanish brackets protruding from its eaves. The plan was the traditional hacienda one—a large interior courtyard surrounded by building on three sides and a wall, in this case with entry steps, closing off the fourth side. The side facades are austere and reveal an influence in fenestration from McKim, Mead, and White, while the rear facade is crowded and disjuncted. Mizner was still formulating his thoughts and learning his profession; there is no doubt.

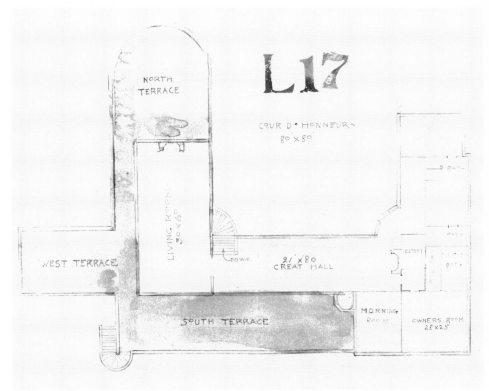

Early Version of the First Floor Plan for a Beach House for Mrs. O. H. P. Belmont, Great Neck, L.I., 1915. Pencil and watercolor on drafting tissue.

Drawings for a Spanish beach house, designed in 1915, for Mrs. O. H. P. Belmont at Great Neck, Long Island show a stylistic maturation.[14] Two versions of the house exist and it is difficult to decipher the final design. The site must have had a quick, steep drop to the beach, which Mizner capitalized upon, in the fashion of his earlier Russian Hill home—a tall facade on the beach, a lower one on the land side. The house was to be built of rubble and concrete with a tile roof. Mizner showed his concern for functionalism. He designed the house to have maximum views of the ocean and he positioned it to catch the morning light and the sea breezes. The first floor was reserved for servants' quarters, storage rooms and a spacious courtyard, "cour d'honneur", which measured 76' x 78' and provided a grand entrance to an external, enclosed stair which led to the main (second) floor. That floor contained a great hall, a dining room, a cloistered passage, a large garden, kitchens, and spacious bedrooms, while on the third floor were the master bedroom, with a spectacular view, smaller bedrooms, and many terraces. Large rooms were the order. Privacy for the guests and the master of the house was built into the design.

It is possible to draw some conclusions from this residence in reference to Mizner's fully-developed style. First, it should be clarified that not all architects have styles which develop, but Mizner very clearly did. He was almost always involved with Spanish and its adaptation and modernization with an emphasis on the individual creativity of the architect who, after all, was a living American, not a Medieval monk, and who therefore had different concerns, functioned under different constraints, and had different goals. Mizner was very conscious of the effect of entrance into a building. He often employed focal points, in this case the exterior stair, a typically Spanish motif, which complimented what were otherwise rather unadorned, simple, clean-lined facades. The visitor was lured across the expansive courtyard. Once within the stair the scale changed and a sense of security, belying the manorial aspect of the building, took over. Then at the end one spilled out into the impressive great hall, its grandeur maximized by this new shift in scale. The pattern of design — focal point, personal scale, and shift to a grand scale — is typical of Mizner.

Mizner's architectural practice was progressing smoothly, "...time flashed by, as my business increased", [15] until the outbreak of World War I when there was a tremendous national slump in building and then his practice dwindled to almost nothing. His beloved mother died. His leg was seriously reinjured in a robbery attempt and the severe fuel shortage of 1917 was making his bed-ridden life intolerable. Change was imperative.

1 Addison Mizner, *The Many Mizners*, Sears Publishing Co., New York City, 1932, p. 241 and p. 244.

2 Mizner's design scrapbooks are in the Mizner Collection at the Society of the Four Arts Library, Palm Beach, Florida. There are many scrapbooks on varied subjects compiled between 1905 and 1933.

3 *The Many Mizners*, p. 247.

4 "Later buildings" refers to the design period 1882-1906. See for example the Villard Residence, Madison Avenue between 50th and 51st Sts., New York City, of 1882-1886. Harry Thaw shot Stanford White in 1906.

5 Mizner scrapbook, "Greece, Rome, Italy", Mizner Collection of the Society of the Four Arts Library, n.p.

6 *Scrapbook*, "Greece, Rome, Italy", n.p.

7 *The Many Mizners*, p. 252.

8 *Ibid.*, p. 253.

9 *Trow's General Directory of New York City*, Polk, Inc., New York City, 1908, p. 1007. This directory was consulted for the years 1893 to 1918.

10 *The Many Mizners*, p. 252 and *Dau's New York Blue Book*, Dau Publishing Co., New York City, for the years 1911 to 1914.

11 The Hotel Rand is still standing at 142 W. 49th St. and although radically altered since Mizner's work, the clientele has remained similar. Wilson Mizner operated the hotel for opium-smoking friends and female visitors. Longtime employees in the area remembered a "beautiful central fountain" in the lobby with entrances to the hotel from both cross streets.

12 "Old Cow Bay Manor House", *Architectural Record*, March 1917, no pages.

13 Drawings in the Collection of The Historical Society of Palm Beach County.

14 Drawings in the Collection of The Historical Society of Palm Beach County.

15 *The Many Mizners*, p. 287.

Mizner came with Paris Singer, as his house guest, to Palm Beach on January 3, 1918. Having visited the island in 1908 with friends, Mizner's opinion on that trip of the early architecture was basically honest, "...there was nothing but two old wooden Flagler hotels".[1] Most visitors to Palm Beach lived in the hotels, as the "season" was extremely short, January 2nd to February 22nd, and the hotels offered conveniences unavailable to individual homeowners in what was still essentially an isolated community. The houses which had been built were in northern styles — predominantly "shingle style" houses with deep porches — and not particularly well-adapted to the southern climate.[2] Mizner found them architecturally satisfactory but completely out of place in a semi-tropical setting:

Northern architecture didn't register. I couldn't get away from that fact. There was one New England Colonial house that was placed in the midst of cocoanut trees and it was an abortion. The house wasn't bad — it had good simplicity — but in Florida it was out of the picture. It couldn't hold its own in that strong color and light, and, with the cocoanut trees hanging over the front door, it certainly looked absurd.[3]

By 1918 the picture had begun to alter. Smaller development houses in the California bungalow style were beginning to spring up in the Poinciana Park Subdivision. More important to the growth of Palm Beach as a residential community was the inability of Americans to visit the Riviera which was closed because of World War I. Wealthy Americans had for almost one hundred years gone off to the famous hotels and spas of the south coast of France and of Monaco. There were many distinguished residences owned by Americans on the European Riviera. With this playground inaccessible, Americans turned to Palm Beach and its Flagler hotels. The community grew and prospered, while merchants and hostelers alike struggled to develop the image of Palm Beach as the American Riviera.

Paris Singer was among the wealthy Americans ousted from Europe by the War. He had turned his homes in France and near London into troop hospitals.[4] Arriving in New York City, he sent for the head nurse of his London hospital to care for Mizner and to begin plans for a hospital to be built in the United States for our convalescing officers. The selection of Palm Beach as the site for such a hospital was an astute one. Singer was a man of luxury and he recognized the potential of Palm Beach, having visited it previously with the idea of building a dance school for his beloved Isadora Duncan.[5] It was a good place for soldiers to revitalize, for Singer to relax, and for an investment to yield solid returns.

Together Mizner and Singer selected the Lake Worth site for the Everglades Club and for legal purposes they formed the Ocean and Lake Realty Company with Mizner as its salaried president.[6] Upon seeing the site, Mizner, in an utterly romantic moment, described what he would build:

...it ought to be something religious — a nunnery, with a chapel built into the lake, with a great cool cloisters and a court of oranges; a landing stage, where the stern old abbess could barter with boatmen bringing their fruit and vegetables for sale; a great gate over there on the road, where the faithful could leave their offerings and receive largess.[7]

Contention must have been immediate for at first Singer did not envision a permanent structure. The persuasive Mizner wrote:

It took me sometime to convince Paris it would be better to build something well; that is, out of fireproof construction instead of a makeshift. It was the first of July [1918] before we had decided to do something that could be used as a club when the war was over. Finally, he okehed (sic) a very rough sketch of the Everglades Club.... The afternoon of his departure we roughly staked out the main building. It was the tenth or twelfth of July.[8]

The Everglades Club from Lake Worth (west facade), ca. 1920. (Sam R. Quincey)

Mizner wanted to design in his Spanish mode for Florida. He had ideas for Palm Beach. He threw himself into the design and construction of the Everglades Club — teaching men to make tiles, others how to read plans, flagging down passing dredges and sweet-talking their operators into a little job on the sly. He turned Joe's Alligator Farm, a muddy, mosquito-infested quagmire into the Everglades Club in six months, a phenomenal undertaking with unskilled labor and with severe wartime shortages of construction materials.

The gouache drawing of the Everglades Club (colorplate 2), signed and dated "Addison Mizner 1918", must have been one of the earliest schemes for the hospital/club. The Orange Court with its backdrop of simple arches and central tower was a part of his first verbalized concept. In all his buildings Mizner liked indoor/outdoor spaces, areas where the outside and inside became one by opening a series of windows or doors, as seen to the left in the early sketch. Interesting is the switch in color mid-way on the building facade, a switch actually carried out.[9]

Construction was of hollow tile with stucco walls and red-tiled roofs. The interior of the Club provided spacious rooms with boxed pecky cypress beams which were internally supported with steel, bowing therefore being an aesthetic ruse rather than a structural deficiency.[10] In November, 1918 the *Palm Beach Weekly News* described the Club complex then still under construction:

As the colony now stands there are seven cottages, each, outside the coloring, identical with the other. Tiled roof and stucco, each of seven rooms with private bath, a servant's room and kitchenette. The rooms and porches are so arranged that a private porch or sun parlor, is allotted every room. The doctor's house, with its exercising, waiting, consulting and operating rooms, has also sleeping accommodations for the doctor and two nurses.... The Clubhouse, representing a thirteenth century Spanish castle (sic) and medieval throughout, is a study in Moorish and Italian, blended indiscriminately to the result desired. Of course in luxury of appointments, the modern is in evidence, rest rooms for the ladies, hair dressing parlors, etc. Barber shops, regulation hotel desks, telephone booths and all the best offerings of the finest of hotel service is at the club guests command. The sleeping accommodations include twelve rooms with bath and two suites to be occupied by Mr. Singer and Mr. Mizner, respectively. The great club room, with its mammoth 7-foot fireplaces and old Moorish rafters (sic) with designs in harmony, are bound to produce an atmosphere that Mr. Mizner is striving to attain. Then there is the dining room with a seating capacity of three hundred persons and jutting out into the lake is a 30 foot terrace where one may dine and watch the gondolas glide over the moonlit canal down to the city of Venice. We come back to reality.[11]

The Lake Worth (west) facade of the Everglades Club is atypical of Mizner's work, for although flat and heavily fenestrated, its curved cornice line and small dome-shaped side towers are reminiscent of old Mexico and its Spanish Colonial religious architecture. The building is stylistically a composite, although not to the bizarre extent suggested by the article above, again with no direct borrowings but with hints of Spanish monuments, as for example the Orange Court inspired by a court of the same name at the Mosque in Seville. All the parts are prototypically Spanish — the private garden cloister, the central tower, the spiral stair on the Worth Avenue facade (ca. 1925); but there are also distinct Mizner departures from the traditional — the freewheeling interior stair, the boat landing, the truss construction of the dining room.

Many Mizner alterations were made to the Everglades Club between 1919 and 1926, as the Club was so popular that expansion was almost constant. In ca. 1919 locker rooms were added to the clubhouse, "connecting with the Loggia, which later has been greatly enlarged and improved".[12] A garage with servants' quarters and parking for one hundred cars was built opposite the clubhouse. All the public rooms were redecorated; the medical villa reinstalled with thirteen bedrooms for bachelors; and the main building altered to "fourteen suites, consisting of two bedrooms and a bathroom to accommodate married men and their wives."[13] After refurbishment in 1921, the seven lodge buildings came to be known as the "maisonettes". One maisonette is described in the March 22, 1921 issue of *Palm Beach Life*:

The lower floor [has been] given over to a block of artistic shops which have proven a great convenience as well as a valuable adjunct to this section of the resort, while the upper floors have been converted into most artistic apartments. . . . The entrance to the apartments is from Alamanda Walk — a terrace twelve feet wide which is almost entirely covered with Alamandas and other beautiful tropical plants. The building contains nine four-room apartments consisting of two bedrooms, two baths, sitting room and maid's room and three eight-room apartments.[14]

With the signing of the 1918 Armistice, Mizner was afraid that his architectural career in Palm Beach had ended;

but Paris Singer, bolstered by his financial resources, had a vision which was dependent upon the genius of Mizner. To the architect's fears Singer responded, "If we start things off right, it will make Palm Beach the winter capital of the world. There is no place in Europe to compare with the climate; all that is needed is to make it gay and attractive. It's up to you and me".[15]

To describe all of Mizner's architecture between 1918 and 1933 would be excessive. A list of buildings and projects is provided at the end of this essay. It is much more important that the reader understand Mizner's design philosophy and then, informed, look at Mizner buildings with that philosophy in mind.

Mizner wanted to transform Palm Beach. He disliked the wooden buildings, finding them northern, alien, and unsuited to their tropical surroundings. He overlooked the modern Villa Zilla which Frank Lloyd Wright had designed on the ocean in 1912. Mizner was at heart a nineteenth-century classicist who admired refinement and gracious elegance in architecture. He was pragmatic enough to realize that modern society had demands not answered by sixteenth and seventeenth century buildings. He also recognized that to copy was to stultify and nowhere in his architecture did Mizner ever copy directly. At times it can be said that he was inspired by specific architectural parts. For example, the main staircase of the Stotesbury Residence bore an initial resemblance to the Golden Stair of the Cathedral at Burgos. But to spend time searching for historical precedents is to miss the point and beauty of his design.

Mizner succinctly stated his architectural philosophy in an interview for *Arts and Decoration*:

There should be no mechanics in art. Art should be a restful thing — a state of mind where one has forgotten a T-square and the dividers. Ninety percent of the beautiful old things in Europe were done before machinery was invented. In those days architectural

The Everglades Club from Worth Ave., 1918-1926 (north facade). (Craig Kuhner, 1977)

forms were cut out by hand and by eye. Everything in a house should be made a part of the harmony of restful pleasing lines.[16]

Mizner has been chastised for "changing things when building" and "working without plans". The latter accusation is untrue. Extant drawings indicate that each building had an extensive set of plans. It seems that Mizner would do a watercolor, gouache, or quick pencil sketch of an idea for a building and turn it over to be further designed, drawn, planned, and orchestrated by his very competent architectural staff. Mizner might consult his design scrapbooks for ideas. One of his chief architects has commented, "Mr. Mizner had innate perspective. He worked with his imagination from pictures". [17] Initial plans and elevations would be drawn up, usually for Mizner's personal inspection. When approved, and there are frequently corrections or changes written in by Mizner, the architects and draftsmen assigned to that specific job drew up finished elevations and plans and did drawings for important architectural details, often to ¼ inch or even full-scale.

Construction would then begin with Mizner frequently visiting the site, teaching skills, supervising delicate work, and making, usually minor, design changes as the building was going up. Windows might be lowered, a balcony added, or in one instance an entire floor was inserted.[18] But changes in buildings under construction are never uncommon when the architect is present on the site. It should also be realized that construction was extraordinarily quick. Building for a forty-room residence usually began in March or April and the house was to be open, completely decorated and landscaped, by the following January. This was an enormous feat for Mizner who was sometimes working on six major residences at once and who often had to rely upon unskilled labor with building materials in short supply. It is primarily for these reasons as well as his love for handcrafted products in a building that Mizner formed Mizner Industries which supplied him with roof and floor tiles, stonework, furniture, wrought iron, pottery, and glasswork.

The reasons for Mizner's selection of the old architecture of Spain as a basis, and he himself used the word "basis", are clearly stated in the *Arts and Decoration* interview:

I based my design largely on the old architecture of Spain — with important modifications to meet Florida conditions and modern ways of living. I studied the architecture of Spain itself and drew somewhat on my knowledge of Spanish tropical America. Architects today try too much to copy from each other, instead of absorbing the best of the old world and letting it run out of their pencils. The old art has withstood the criticism of centuries.[19]

It is also true that Mizner worked in a simplified Venetian Gothic style, most obviously in the "Casa de Leoni" for Len Thomas, and in a rustic half-timbered Spanish, most apparent in the Paul Moore residence. Mizner knew that his clients who were either members of the aristocracy or of the *nouveau riche* were conservative in their tastes. But that is precisely why Mizner was a success in Florida. He too was conservative. He recognized the pleasure the wealthy took in nostalgic, romantic images of Europe because he shared their same memories. But, Mizner's love of Spanish architecture went far deeper. His personal library, which remains intact at the Society of the Four Arts Library, is one of the best possible on Spanish and Spanish Colonial architecture and decorative arts.[20] Mizner was brilliant at his own version of twentieth-century Spanish because he innately understood Romanesque, sixteenth, and seventeenth century design. He knew it so well that it was a part of his mind, heart, and soul.

Mizner also had analyzed the peculiarities of designing in Florida and he stated some of his responses to those peculiarities:

...I adapted Spanish architecture to Florida — with color, lots of color. There is a very strong light down there, reflected from the

North Elevation, Residence for Leonard Thomas, "Casa de Leoni", Palm Beach, 1920. Ink on glossy linen.

East Elevation, Residence for Leonard Thomas, "Casa de Leoni", Palm Beach, 1920. Ink on glossy linen.

South Elevation, Residence for Leonard Thomas, "Casa de Leoni", Palm Beach, 1920. Ink on glossy linen.

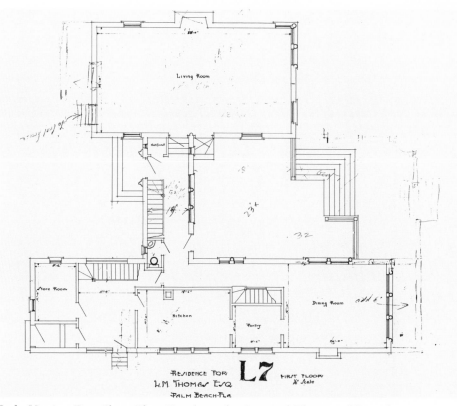

Early Version First Floor Plan, Residence for Leonard Thomas, "Casa de Leoni", Palm Beach, 1920. Ink on glossy linen.

sands, and the ocean glistens like an opal, with pinks, blues, and greens. I used all sorts of pastel colors on the exterior of my houses to kill the glare—nearly always choosing light and transparent rather than the more sombre colors of the North.[21]

Mizner is a master of color which was an essential component of his architecture. Watercolors were always used to create delicate hues which changed with the light. The exterior of the Cosden house was cream which "be[came] shaded with the rising and setting of the sun, reflecting the brilliant white light in a delicate amber, pink, saffron, and old wine."[22] A description of the Mesker house is even more intriguing:

The Mesker house is finished in a sober color that defies classification. At certain perspectives it assumes the aspect of

Bookplate, Addison Mizner. (Lee Brian)

South Facade, Residence for Gurnee Munn, Palm Beach, 1919. (Craig Kuhner, 1977)

a mottled purple. At others it will be a decided grey color, with a tinge of indigo in it. Under the brilliant sunlight it assumes a more springlike color shining in a colorful brilliance. The roof in this instance is complementary too, it carries the shading into a sober finale of color. In this home the use of small ornamentation is most effective. Where the dark could become too somber, a live touch of color is imparted by a bowl of artificial fruit in terra cotta, or by a small coat of arms or other colorful motif.[23]

Since after fifty years no original paints remain on the exterior of Mizner buildings, an original ceiling (colorplate 4) gives the most accurate glimpse at Mizner's color sense. The native pecky cypress is highlighted by soft celadon and moss green with accents of umber and sienna. The result is powerful but not oppressive.

Facades of Mizner buildings are simple and flat, usually pierced by almost haphazard groupings of windows of different styles. Flatness is emphasized. Shallow set-backs range across a long facade to create a quiet movement along the surface. The only distraction is a strong architectural motif, sometimes an ornate entryway as in the "Casa de Leoni" or a mirador with the top floor heavily-windowed as in the Villa Mizner or an external stair as in the Rasmussen and many other residences. These architectural attractions are focal points which are meant to intrigue and involve the visitor in the structure. Lester Geisler described the Rasmussen stair in particular:

I remember Mizner's sketch. He started with a big circle. Why he did I don't know. Maybe he had talked with Mrs. Rasmussen and sold her the big stair. But he started with a circle. Then he worked his rooms around it. I was the office steerer for that particular job. It came to me then, being the engineer, to make it stand up. The workmen who put up the stair were afraid it would fall down. It hasn't yet. There is no central support. You don't need it. You build around in a circle. It's like building an arch, every step holds every other step. It's confined with concrete and steel or it would fly out. Your reinforcement is a spiral.[24]

Mizner found baroque architecture overornamented for Florida and thus he concentrated on special attractions played against flat, tall facades.[25] Just as the background for architecture intrigued him in Guatemala, so too it was a concern for him in Florida:

...Florida is flat as a pancake. You must build with a strong skyline to give your building character, you must get effects

West Facade, Residence for George Rasmussen, Palm Beach, 1924. (Craig Kuhner, 1977)

Interior of External Stair, Residence for George Rasmussen, Palm Beach, 1924. (Craig Kuhner, 1977)

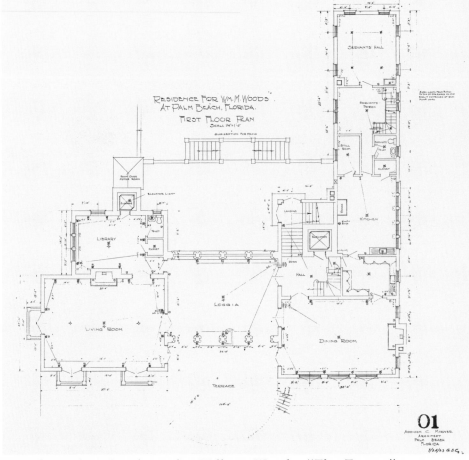

First Floor Plan, Residence for William Woods, "The Towers", Palm Beach, 1923. Pencil on drafting tissue.

with changes in level of a few feet, as in the case of gardens and terraces.

...in a flat site, a house must have stronger interest than where it is a spot against a big landscape background. The landscape gives you no help in Florida. You must make your own.[26]

A particularly dynamic skyline is seen in "The Towers" built in 1923 for William M. Woods. Miradors of varying heights, some reaching five stories, vie with one another against the backdrop of a Florida sky. The eastern Mexican church facade of the Everglades Club is strong, particularly against an early morning sky. The Boca Raton Cloister seems Medieval with its lacey pinnacles set against the rich oranges and pinks of a sunset.

The typical Mizner residence had an austere facade with an architectural detail as a focal point and an interior courtyard, designed on a very human scale. This courtyard or patio usually had several entrance points from public rooms which ranged along one or two sides and from a hallway or cloisterway which gave access to groundfloor bedrooms. The public rooms were spacious, light-filled with many windows which opened for breeze and view. Almost every residence had a living room, a loggia room, a dining room, and a

Loggia Room and Cloisterway, Residence for William Gray Warden, Palm Beach, 1922. (Craig Kuhner, 1977)

library with the orientation discussed above. The loggia room usually had windows which recessed completely into floors or walls on three sides. The room could become almost an enclosed patio and it could be considered the forerunner of the Florida room. Houses were designed for entertaining with public rooms adjacent and accessible via wide doorways. Most residences were used as beach houses and thus Mizner designed baths, often with showers, to either side of the main entrance door. The loggia rooms, double baths, and cloisterways with heavily-glazed columned walls can be considered trademarks of Mizner interiors.

Usually the first floor had at least two guest rooms with more provided on the second floor along with family bedrooms. Almost without exception bedrooms were very simple with private or adjoining baths. Master bedrooms often had fireplaces; guest rooms sometimes had kidney-warmer fireplaces, small nichelike fireplaces set at kidney

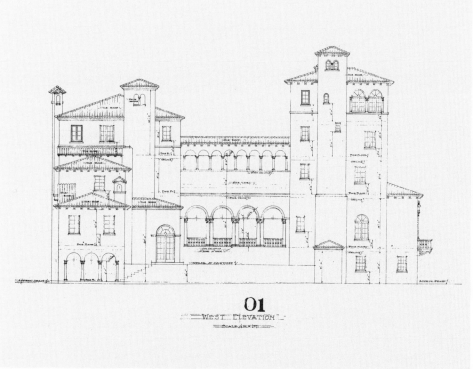
West Elevation, Residence for William Woods, "The Towers", Palm Beach, 1923. Pencil on drafting tissue.

Entryhall, Residence for William Gray Warden, Palm Beach, 1922. (Craig Kuhner, 1977)

South Facade, Residence for Paul Moore, Palm Beach, 1924. (Craig Kuhner, 1977)

Main entrance, Villa Mizner, Via Mizner 1924. (Craig Kuhner, 1977)

Dining Room, Residence for William Gray Warden,
Palm Beach, 1922. Addison Mizner, Architect. Floor
Tiles and Door by Mizner Industries.
(Craig Kuhner, 1977)

31

Orange Court, The Everglades Club, Palm Beach, 1918. Signed lower right, "Addison Mizner 1918". Gouache on paper. Lent by The Everglades Club. (Lee Brian)

Bathroom of Paris Singer, The Everglades Club, Palm Beach, 1918. Addison Mizner, Architect. (Craig Kuhner, 1977)

Ceiling, Residence for William Gray Warden, Palm Beach, 1922. Addison Mizner, Architect. (Craig Kuhner, 1977)

Main Facade, Riverside Baptist Church, Jacksonville, Fla., 1926. Addison Mizner, Architect. (Craig Kuhner, 1977)

Interior, Riverside Baptist Church, Jacksonville, Fla., 1926.
Addison Mizner, Architect. (Craig Kuhner, 1977)

level in a wall. Master bathrooms could be quite ornate (color-plate 2) with colorful patterns of Mizner Industries tiles, usually in Mizner Blue with black and/or Mizner Yellow. Second floors had many balconies and terraces which had romantic water, courtyard, and red-tiled roof views. Servants' rooms were normally over the kitchen wing or the garage.

Kitchens were important to Mizner because they were important to his clients. He stressed that kitchens should be spacious with much pantry and preparation space and, above all, that they should be downwind. His kitchens were quite modern — special refrigeration rooms, flower arranging rooms, hotel-size cast-iron gas stoves, many cupboards, silver drawers, serving rooms, and turn-a-round servers. But as pragmatic and as functional as Mizner was, he still recognized the kitchen's place within his design concept:

Now, one point of house design is, that you must have the utmost perfection in the service and then the instant you pass on the other side of the pantry door, you should enter into something that is restful and attractive and as far away from the mechanics as you can get. There you want art.[27]

To Mizner architecture meant far more than the exterior and plan of a building. He saw architecture as an integration of the structure, its interior decoration, and its landscaping. To ensure that the interior furnishings harmonized with his architectural design, Mizner required that clients permit him to decorate at least the first floor of their building. Mizner Industries, which is discussed in the last section of this catalogue, played a key role in the decoration.

Landscaping, which was often sub-contracted, was still initially planned by Mizner and the architectural firm. Swimming pools, garden fountains, garden walls and gates, coral stone patios and steps, flowered terraces, all emanated from the architect. Native plants and trees were used against native pecky cypress, brain coral, and patterned Spanish and Miz-

Coralstone Garden Wall with Pecky Cypress Gate, Residence for Paul Moore, Palm Beach, 1924. (Craig Kuhner, 1977)

ner Blue tiles. The whole idea was to accent semi-tropical Florida and to fortify the indoor/outdoor aspects of Mizner's buildings.

Mizner's busiest design years were 1921-25, although he never suffered for commissions after the Everglades Club. It is impossible to fully reconstruct the Mizner firm, but there were a few chief architects and several trusted draftsmen over the years. Lester Geisler, who later designed the Hialeah racetracks, was a designer for Mizner from 1923-26 and an "associate" from 1928-31. Byron Simonson, who was later responsible for much of the development of Hilton Head, worked with Mizner in the mid-1920's and returned to design for him in 1931. Principal draftsmen, including structural advisors, and possible designers were: Adrian Barragan-Dorcas, Luis Barragan-Dorcas, A.E.R. Betschick, and T.P. Davis. In 1925 there were no less than twenty-one different draftsmen's signatures on drawings from the Mizner firm.[28]

Cloister, Worth Ave., Palm Beach, 1924 (Craig Kuhner, 1977).

In 1924 and 1925 Mizner completed the Via Mizner and the Via Parigi respectively. These two shopping alleys at the west end of Worth Avenue are perfect examples of the func-

tionalism of Mizner's architecture. They remain fundamentally unchanged after fifty years.[29] The combination of public walkway, commercial space, and private residence creates the excitement of the Vias. At each turn there was a new discovery—a garden spot with a restaurant, an overhanging balcony laden with bougainvillea, a tiled stairway surprisingly tucked beneath a bridge, and always little shops to tantalize.

Mizner's own residence occupied the mirador or tower on Worth Avenue. The bridge over Via Mizner connected the hallway of his home to the drafting studio. The main floor of Mizner's villa is on the second floor with access by elevator and stair from a massive doorway and porch on the Via Mizner. The paneled dining room and the large living room are joined by a vaulted hallway.[30] A totally private terrace overlooked Worth Avenue. Bedrooms occupied the third and fourth floors, while in the single fifth floor room Mizner had a spacious study for designing and reading. Structurally, the building is very sound, with extremely thick walls to hold the height.

The genius of the Vias is that they not only create intimacy but also generate movement. The visitor is immediately at ease and no matter how frantic upon entrance to a Via he slackens his pace and begins to stroll at leisure. The Vias and the shops within the cloistered arcade on Worth Avenue seem separate from the rest of Palm Beach. They become their own village. The buildings are tall, then low; with intricate stonework, then utterly plain; and all seem compressed and condensed. Mizner described their quintessence:

This is the charming Via Mizner—a row of tiny shops at Palm Beach, with the picturesqueness of Old Spain—the narrow streets of Granada. Characteristic also, are the light stucco walls, in pastel tints, topped with the tile roofs and weathered cypress woodwork, and the inevitable cocoanut tree with its decorative tufted shape and play of light and shade against the stucco wall.[31]

1 Addison Mizner, *The Many Mizners*, Sears Publishing Co., New York City, 1932, p. 263.

2 For an outstanding analysis of northern architectural styles of the period see Vincent Scully, *The Shingle Style and the Stick Style: Architectural Theory and Design from Richardson to the Origins of Wright*, Yale University Press, New Haven, 1971. For the early development of Palm Beach consult The Junior League of the Palm Beaches, *Palm Beach Entertains: Then and Now*, Coward, McCann & Geoghegan, Inc., New York City, 1976 and Barbara D. Hoffstot, *Landmark Architecture of Palm Beach*, Ober Park Associates Inc., Pittsburgh, 1974.

3 "The Florida House", an interview of Addison Mizner by John Taylor Boyd, *Arts and Decoration*, January 1930, Vol. 32, pp. 39-40.

4 Paris Singer was an heir to the Singer sewing machine fortune. He had always lived in Europe prior to the outbreak of the War. See Isadora Duncan, *My Life*, Liveright Publishing Corporation, New York City, 1955.

5 Addison Mizner, Incomplete Manuscript, ca. 1932, Private Collection, p. 3 and *My Life*, p. 331.

6 *Mizner Incomplete Manuscript*, p. 30.

7 *Ibid.*, pp. 29-30.

8 *Ibid.*, p. 35.

9 Members of the Everglades Club who remember the building from 1919 believe this to be the case. They may recall an optical illusion created by the sun at certain times of the day.

10 In the Sea Island Club (1928) Mizner completed the roof and then constructed an artificial ridge to make it appear to sag. Interview with Lester Geisler, Kissimmee, Florida, May, 1976.

11 *Palm Beach Weekly News*, November 1, 1918, pp. 1, 10.

12 *Palm Beach Weekly News*, December 19, 1919, p. 1.

13 *Ibid.*

14 "The Everglades Club", *Palm Beach Life*, March 22, 1921, pp. 14-15.

15 *Mizner Incomplete Manuscript*, p. 40.

16 *Arts and Decoration*, p. 36.

17 *Interview with Lester Geisler.*

18 Elevation Drawing for Buildings Nos. 5, 6, 7, Via Parigi, Addison Mizner Architect, n.d., Private Collection.

19 *Arts and Decoration*, p. 40.

20 Mizner's architectural reading was extensive and eclectic. Included in his library were such books as *European Arms and Armor, Dutch Tiles of the Fifteenth to Eighteenth Centuries, The Art of the Plasterer*, and *Picturesque China: Architecture and Landscape*, to name but a few of the more intriguing non-Spanish items. From his scrapbook clippings it is apparent that Mizner read all of the major architectural journals.

21 *Arts and Decoration*, p. 40.

22 "Spanish Architecture", *Palm Beach Life*, February 17, 1925, p. 22.

23 *Ibid.*

24 *Interview with Lester Geisler.*

25 *Arts and Decoration*, p. 40.

26 *Ibid.*

27 *Ibid.*, p. 36.

28 For a complete list of signatures and initials found on the drawings in the Collection of The Historical Society of Palm Beach County consult that organization.

29 The area with buildings behind the main drafting studio and opposite the entrance to the Villa Mizner was originally an open patio. The fountain in Via Parigi is not original and the recent renovation to that alley has involved some painting of Mizner stonework.

30 Mizner used to joke that his living room ceiling in the Villa Mizner was two feet too low because if he ever had to install a floor in the middle to make apartments, it couldn't be done. *Interview with Lester Geisler.*

31 *Arts and Decoration*, p. 36.

⋀⋀ 1925-1933

The dream lay in Boca Raton. Mizner, frustrated by the rapid development of Palm Beach and lured by the prospect of designing his own complete town, developed his dream for Boca Raton.[1] The scheme for Boca Raton was ideal, but not idealistic, at least not for the boom year of 1925. Mizner had had tremendous successes in Palm Beach, was known nationally as an architect, and had the financial support of some of the richest people in the country.

Mizner Development Corporation, the legal developer of Boca Raton, advertised:

Boca Raton is not an addition — however worthy — to an already existing community. It is not a suburban development — however distinguished — of a crowded commercial center. It is a cosmopolitan world-community — destined to be the world's most architecturally beautiful playground.[2]

Mizner envisioned a luxury hotel with golf courses on the mainland side of the Boca Raton Inlet, large homes and a second hotel along the strip of oceanland, and a splendid highway to approach this opulent community. He also planned his own castle home for a small island to be reached by drawbridge. There was to be a jockey club, polo fields, an air strip, and even a floating restaurant designed as a Caravelle.[3] A magnificent cathedral dedicated to the memory of "Mama Mizner" was to be the best work Mizner had ever done. Dreams must be made before they can become realities.

The *Distrito de Boca Raton* was to be a restricted residential community. Requirements for this area were quite stringent — acceptance for property purchase was theoretically by a social committee, ocean houses had to cost $40,000, second tier homes $30,000 and all others $20,000.[4]

But Mizner was also pragmatic and realized that his hotels and mansions needed a support system. He planned housing for the service staff, a residential development (Floresta) for the management and community leaders, a

RESIDENCE OF ADDISON MIZNER AT LAKE BOCA RATON. THE ENTRANCE ACROSS THE DRAWBRIDGE INTO THE FORECOURT

Sketch for a Castle Residence for Addison Mizner, Boca Raton, 1925. (Photograph courtesy of Boca Raton Cloisters)

water tower, two railroad stations, a town hall, a radio station, and he even reserved a section for "factory", presumably a subdivision of *Las Manos*.[5] The plan was a comprehensive one. All buildings were to be in the Spanish style — an architecturally, aesthetically cohesive community.

Mizner recognized that he could not design all of Boca Raton, but as Mizner Development Corporation advertisements pointed out, "No structure, large or small, can be erected in Boca Raton without the approval of Addison Mizner".[6] Acreage had to be sold to the small home developer as well, and even small investors wanted something for their money. Advertisements clearly stated:

Boca Raton will surpass in exclusiveness any resort on Florida's East Coast. But the democracy of Addison Mizner has provided large and well-selected bathing beaches, golf course, and tennis courts, aviation field, polo ground and dock rights for the use of all. The most modest home builder in Boca Raton is assured an enjoyment of life in every way equal to that of its largest and most elaborate estate owner.[7]

The dream was partially fulfilled. El Camino Real, a 160 foot wide highway with a central canal patterned after the Botofago in Rio de Janiero, was completed. The Boca Raton Ritz-Carlton on the oceanfront was never begun, but the Ritz-Carlton Cloister on the mainland was opened in February, 1926. The hotel was quite severe with an exceedingly flat facade. The principal ornamentation was the lacey Gothic pinnacles which ran the length of the roofline. The entrance was a magnificent arch of simple line on squat columns, reminiscent of the Romanesque.[8] A central tower gave lift to the structure. The plan had public rooms for dining and relaxation running from the entrance east to the water, with one hundred bedrooms above and on the wing running north and south. The structure perched on the edge of the lake.

East Facade, Ritz-Carlton Cloister, Boca Raton, 1925. (Photograph courtesy of Boca Raton Cloisters)

West Facade, Ritz-Carlton Cloister, Boca Raton, 1925. (Craig Kuhner, 1977)

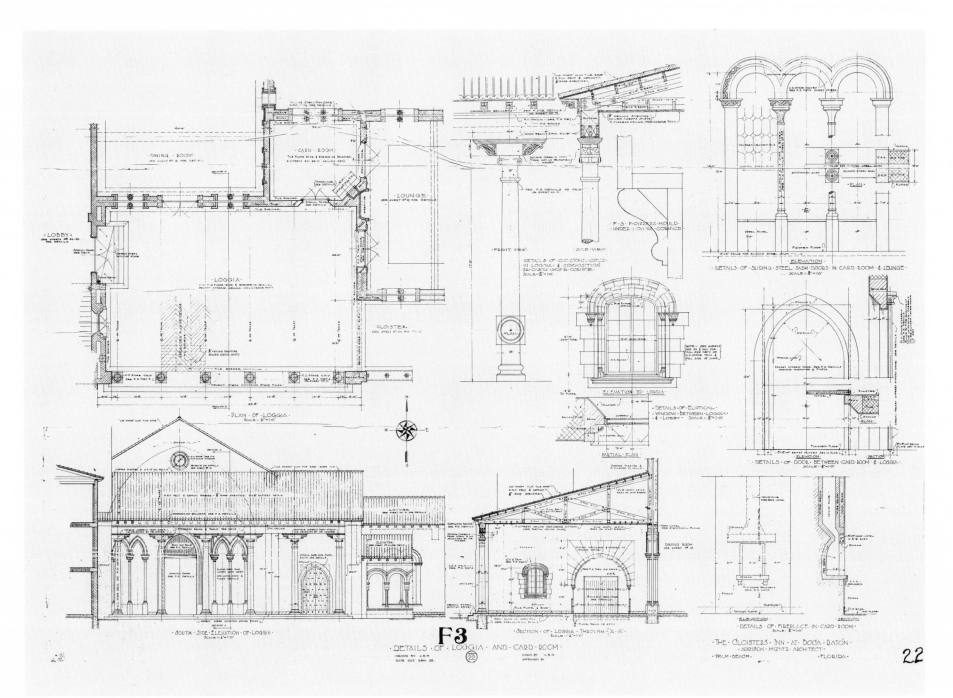

Details of Loggia and Card Room, Ritz-Carlton Cloister, Boca Raton, 1925. Pencil on drafting tissue.

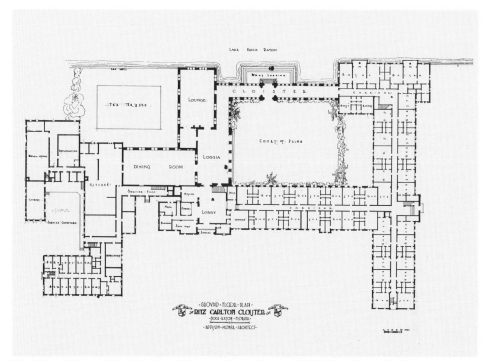

First Floor Plans, Ritz-Carlton Cloister, Boca Raton, 1925. Pencil on drafting tissue.

Main Entrance, West Facade, Ritz-Carlton Cloister, 1925, Boca Raton. (Craig Kuhner, 1977)

Yachts could dock beside a cloisterway to disembark passengers.

The *Distrito de Boca Raton*, the exclusive ocean, lake, and inlet property, had sold well and Mizner had completed designs for several houses, although none were ever constructed.[9] The Administration Building which housed the sales office and chief architects, engineers, and personnel working on the project was completed. It was patterned after El Greco's house in Toledo, a building which even a novice in Spanish architecture could recognize, particularly after being politely slipped the information. The selection was a politic one, although from his design scrapbooks it is apparent that Mizner greatly admired the artist's home.

Sales to smaller home developers must have been healthy. One article reported for the Corporation, "We signed up three different contractors for lots for house building. One bought fifty lots, another sixty-five, and the third two hundred and twenty."[10] Mizner designed small homes for the

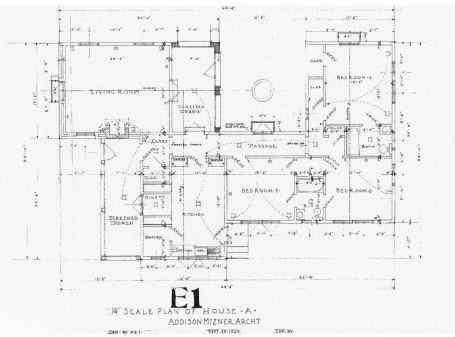

Elevations and Plan for House "A", Housing Development, Boca Raton, 1925. Pencil on drafting tissue.

"Bungalows in the Spanish Manner" designed by Addison Mizner for *The Ladies' Home Journal*, 1927. (Photograph with permission of *The Ladies' Home Journal*)

Druker Development, which was apparently never built. He also designed and constructed a section of Boca Raton called "Floresta". The Reverend Henry Mizner, Addison's older brother, had a two-story house in "Floresta" which was more regal and more customized than those of his neighbors.[11]

The houses of both developments relate to homes designed by Mizner and published in a *Ladies' Home Journal* article, "Bungalows in the Spanish Manner Adapted to American Ideals" of 1927.[12] As in most of the Floresta Development houses, Mizner used only a single-story plan and condensed the rooms, compressing the plan into a square (25' x 25'). The dining room, "fast becoming an unnecessary appendage in very small homes", was replaced by the dining alcove. In one plan Mizner could not force himself to eliminate the central patio, which occupied precious space; in a

Partially Completed Blue Heron Hotel, Singer Island, 1926. (Sam R. Quincey)

second he retained a porch declaring it a fundamental of Spanish design. To be asked by the *Ladies' Home Journal* to submit sketches for small houses was considered by architects to be an honor. Plans and models could be obtained by writing to the editor.

While undertaking his own development at Boca Raton, Mizner was also designing Paris Singer's new project for the uninhabited island across the northern inlet from Palm Beach. Singer had sold his home and the Everglades Club in 1924 to amass capital for his project. Presumably Singer planned a residential development, as well as the Blue Heron Hotel, which was the only building to even begin construction. It was approximately seven stories tall and bizarre in plan, probably as a result of Mizner's effort to provide all of the rooms with ocean views. Most interesting in the Singer Island project was Mizner's design for an aerial ferry to cross the inlet and connect Palm Beach to Singer Island. It was a visionary idea and doubtless an impossible one. Without tongue in cheek it was reported:

The ferry, copied after a famous structure in Europe and similar to a bridge at Duluth, is to cost approximately three-quarters of a million dollars. The span is a hundred and thirty-six feet above

the water, and suspended from this is a transporter ferry accommodating twelve cars...[13]

Both Boca Raton and Singer Island failed when the Florida land market broke in 1926 and the hurricanes of 1926 and 1928 assured their financial failure. It should be realized that, almost without exception, economists and land speculators believed, until the last moment, that the Florida land market was sound, albeit inflated. Mizner was the most respected developer. In 1926 reputable economic commentators wrote, "...Mr. Singer is developing Palm Beach Ocean, and a few miles farther south Mr. Mizner is projecting at Boca Raton, a resort community which is planned to rival Palm Beach not only in beauty but exclusiveness" and "Florida's boom

Sketch of Proposed Aerial Ferry, Singer Island Project, 1926. (Lee Brian)

has only begun."[14] Charles Donald Fox in *The Truth About Florida* proclaimed:

I know Addison Mizner. I know the high ideals which have guided his every activity, and being familiar with his work I know that all who locate in Boca Raton will see promises fulfilled....I am convinced that Boca Raton will rise to a well-merited prominence among the delightful settlements which dot the lower east coast of the newest golden state. Where the rare talents of Mr. Mizner are loaned — there development must come. Addison Mizner is a genius, and though his great gifts have always been known, it is in the role of empire builder that he shall gain his greatest fame.[15]

Even Kenneth L. Roberts who was skeptical of most Florida developers wrote in reference to the development at Boca Raton, "...it is known that Addison Mizner is one of the great architects of America and would refuse to direct any enterprise that would damage his reputation."[16]

Although Mizner was deep in debt and naturally depressed by the failure of his dream, his career was far from over. After 1926 he remained in Palm Beach but made more frequent trips to Carmel, California, where he had purchased a small ranch and built a large home for his niece, Ysabel Chase. Lester Geisler was an "associate" in the firm from 1928 to 1931. Among the many architectural projects in this later period are designs for several clubs, most notably the Sea Island Club in Sea Island, Georgia and the Embassy Club in Palm Beach. There were also plans for the Beauville Beach Club in Windsor, Ontario, and additions to the Fox Chapel Country Club in Pittsburgh. Residences across the country were commissioned. One of Mizner's finest Florida Spanish houses was built in 1929-30 for the Dietrichs in Monteceito (Santa Barbara), California. Mizner had more national commissions than at any other time in his career. Of course, due to the statewide land crash and the stigma of failing at Boca Raton, Mizner's building in Florida was seriously curtailed, but not stopped.

The Gedney house, 1928, in Manalapan was one of his finest, more imaginative homes, although not palatial in size. The canted front was unorthodox and permitted a full view of the entire facade. The site must have particularly pleased Mizner for the Gedney land reached from ocean to lake with a severe drop from a coral ridge. The east facade of the house is flat and long with slight set-backs. An external, enclosed stair occupied the southeast corner. The house has the traditional hacienda plan and the west facade is busy with wooden balconies and covered walkways to capture picturesque views of the brain coral patio and lake. Planted terraces led down to the lake where there is a great sense of height and dominance from the building. The plan is typical of Mizner — a dramatic front hall with bathrooms to either side, a dining room with a great fireplace and coved ceiling to the west with adjoining kitchens and serving rooms, a small library and huge living room to the east. The loggia room is not included, but there is a series of guest rooms off a private hall and a guest bedroom on the first floor. The second floor which is much smaller has more bedrooms reached via the external spiral stair.

In 1931 Byron Simonson rejoined the Mizner firm and was responsible for much of the designing. From this period most remarkable are designs for the Palm Beach Post Office, for a complex of movie theater, hotel, and restaurant in Belle Glade, and for the Williams Residence in St. Petersburg, Florida. Mizner died in February, 1933 and the firm was dissolved after accepted projects were completed.

Mizner's contributions to the architecture of Palm Beach and of Florida are significant. With his innovative architecture which was romantic and yet conservative, witty and yet functional, people began building private residences on a grand scale. Mizner provided the conveniences his clients demanded. He designed with the wealthy in mind. He had an ability to create a building at once hospitable. Each building was distinctive and unique, but never theatrical. As his chief architect observed, "His work fit the place. It did not become

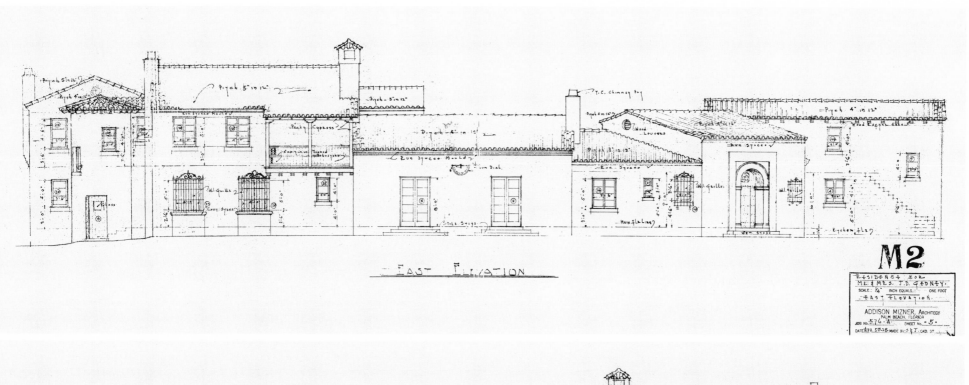

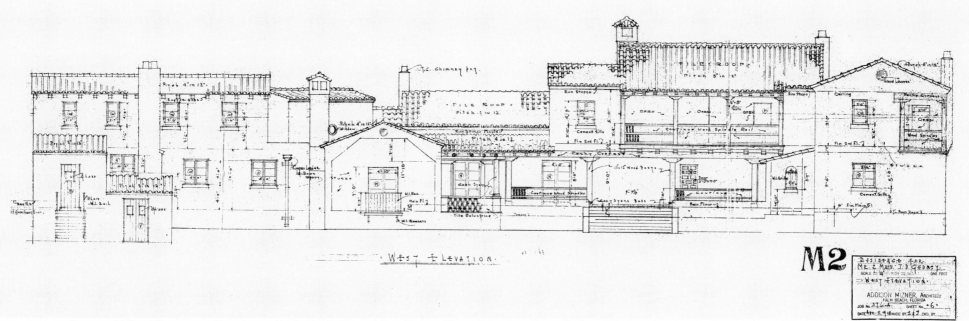

East and West Elevations, Residence for J. D. Gedney, Manalapan, Fla., 1928. Pencil on drafting tissue.

East Facade, Residence for J. D. Gedney, Manalapan, Fla., 1928. (Craig Kuhner, 1977)

tiring. It has an abiding quality."[17]

Palm Beach was transformed. By 1925 Palm Beach had established itself as *the* resort community of the United States. As Arthur Somers Roche attested:

Palm Beach is the most delightful place in the world. I have traveled abroad and seen the French and Italian Riviera. There is no comparison to be drawn between the Cote d'Azur and Palm Beach....To compare it to the Mediterranean resorts would be to their great disadvantage.[18]

More importantly, however, Mizner set the finest example for building in a Spanish style in Florida. Architects and contractors alike copied Mizner, not original Spanish, because Mizner had created a style appropriate to modern Florida. The loggia room has survived as the Florida room. The changing room is now an essential. The focal point, now swimming pool with bridge or hanging basket chair, creates the necessary element of excitement. Native building materials are touted. Red tile remains a precious commodity. Pastel colors prevail. Meandering streets with boutiques are today's key to a successful commercial adventure. The advantages of mixed residential and commercial space have become obvious. And all of this still created in the "Mizner style", as the real estate advertisements and developers' brochures will attest.

In the 1920's Carol Kennicott of *Main Street* and H. L. Mencken, the outstanding observer and wit, agreed on one thing. Carol, depressed by the ugliness of her mid-western town pleaded, "Get a great architect and have him plan a town that would be suitable to the prairie. Perhaps he'd create some entirely new form of architecture. Then tear down all these shambling buildings...."[19] H. L. Mencken acerbically remarked, "I have seen, I believe, all of the most unlovely towns of the world; they are all to be found in the United

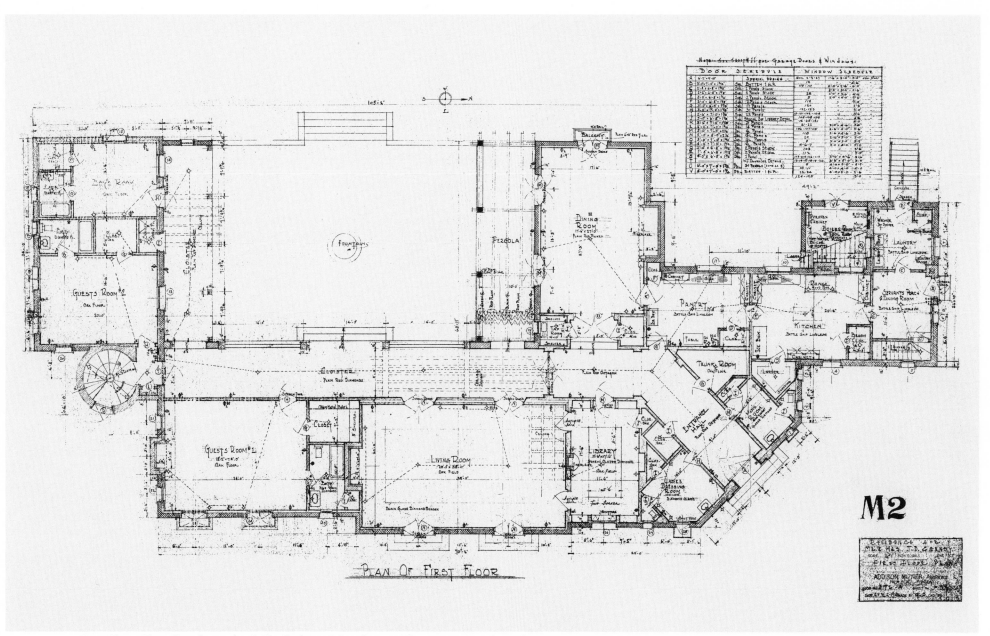

PLAN OF FIRST FLOOR

First Floor Plan, Residence for J. D. Gedney, Manalapan, Fla., 1928. Pencil on drafting tissue.

States."[20] Addison Mizner tried to oblige them by contributing romance, beauty, and unity. For this we owe him our continuing thanks.

▲ 1925-1933 Notes

1 Originally, Mizner planned to build at "Mizner Mile", a strip of ocean-land he had purchased just south of the Lake Worth Inlet, but disheartened by legal problems he moved his project southward. The road was laid out and one house foundation was built. Interview with Karl Riddle, West Palm Beach, Florida, March, 1975 and Interview with Marion Sims Wyeth, Palm Beach, Florida, February, 1975.

2 1926 advertisement for Mizner Development Corporation reprinted through the Courtesy of Fiesta Magazine Archives and Ronald R. McCormick, Boca Raton, Florida, 1976. The "suburban development" probably referred to Merrick's Coral Gables which was rapidly being developed near Miami.

3 Plans in a private collection apparently indicate that a boat for entertaining was designed in 1923 and in another hand on the same drawing the note "Boca Raton" appears. There was a "Spanish galleon" docked in Palm Beach during the mid-1920's, according to Lester Geisler. He believes Mizner designed that boat. Interview with Lester Geisler, Kissimmee, Florida, May, 1976.

4 Mizner Opens Exclusive Area", *Palm Beach Daily News*, January 17, 1926, p. 2, section 1.

5 A large number of drawings for Boca Raton are in the Collection of The Historical Society of Palm Beach County.

6 *1926 advertisement*.

7 *Ibid*.

8 Lester Geisler designed the entrance to the hotel with Mizner's approval. Geisler commented, "I just put together pieces that I knew he liked. He said, 'That's fine'. I don't even know where I got it from; probably from pictures or just thinking that it would look well with the other parts of the building". *Interview with Lester Geisler*.

9 Drawings for this section of Boca Raton can be found in the Collection of The Historical Society of Palm Beach County.

10 "Mizner Project Developing at Rapid Rate Now", *Palm Beach Daily News*, January 2, 1926, p. 11.

11 Twenty-nine houses, including the Reverend Mizner's, still remain from the development.

12 "Bungalows in the Spanish Manner Adapted to American Ideals", *The Ladies' Home Journal*, February, 1927, p. 36.

13 *Palm Beach Daily News*, January 31, 1926, p. 12, section 2.

14 Frank Parker Stockbridge and John Holliday Perry, *Florida in the Making*, The deBower Publishing Co., New York City, 1926, p. 211.

15 Charles Donald Fox, *The Truth About Florida*, no publisher, New York City, 1925, pp. 203-204.

16 Kenneth L. Roberts, *Florida*, Harper & Brothers, New York City, 1926, p. 103.

17 *Interview Lester Geisler*.

18 *Palm Beach Daily News*, January 5, 1925, p. 1. It should be firmly stated that Mizner was not solely responsible for the development of the town in the 1920's. Marion Sims Wyeth, Maurice Fatio, Joseph Urban, and John Volk also designed fine buildings in their own personal Mediterranean styles. Today their buildings are frequently misattributed to Mizner.

19 Sinclair Lewis, *Main Street*, Signet Books, New York City, 10th ed., n.d., p. 139. *Main Street* first appeared in 1920.

20 H. L. Mencken, "The Libido for the Ugly" from *Prejudices*, sixth series, 1927 in *The Vintage Mencken*, ed. by Alistair Cooke, Vintage Books, New York City, 1955, p. 179.

Memorial Fountain, Palm Beach, 1929. (Craig Kuhner, 1977)

⩕ Mizner Industries

With the construction of the Everglades Club in 1918, Addison Mizner was faced with a decision. Should he compromise his architectural design philosophy by building in those shabby materials available to him or should he extend himself as had the Medieval architect to make his own tiles and brick, metal and stonework, — to serve as craftsman and designer? The World War I shipping embargo prevented Mizner from importing handmade roof tiles from abroad and the comparable American roof tile was unacceptable to Mizner who wrote, "All the commercial ones were stamped out and looked like painted tin when they were laid and were a horrible, lurid color, that made a roof look like the floor of a slaughter house."[1] The solution to the dilemma must have been an obvious one for Mizner who had geared his architectural education around observation and for whom inquisition was as important a scholarly tool as the proverbial architectural text. His biographer and friend Ida Tarbell wrote:

In all of his wanderings over the world, studying buildings, looking, sketching, he had never been content until he knew how the thing that attracted him was made....How did the Spaniards get these irregular shapes for their roof tiles? The color of these glazes? That rough surface in the plaster?[2]

Mizner, feeling assured of his expertise, purchased, with the financial aid of Paris Singer, "The Novelty Works" and began his own manufacture of roof and floor tiles with a sideline production of ironwork and furniture.

The company was rudimentary, struggling to produce even the quantity of materials necessary for the construction of the Everglades Club. *Las Manos*, the Spanish word for "handcrafted", was the name for the firm, which was situated in West Palm Beach just east of the railroad.

Clay shipped from Georgia arrived in great quantities. A hoist, kilns, and drying sheds had to be constructed.

Workers had to be trained. The traditional Spanish method of making roof tiles was to bend clay over a man's thigh. However, such a technique results in a very limited number of tiles and unless one is seeking to cover only a small shed within two years time, a more sophisticated method of production is obviously required. The Spanish, therefore, created a wooden form which in shape roughly resembled a man's thigh. It was this more modern, yet still handcrafted, method which Mizner used. When the moist clay had been kneaded, it was spread in a large wooden box or crib. It was smoothed down and cut into rectangular shapes, and then the cut slabs were removed and placed in wooden roof tile forms. These moulds were narrow at one end and had solid wood in the center to create the traditional thigh-shape. The moist clay filled in around the form. After partial drying, the tile was removed and placed in a kiln for baking at 2600° for four days. Color variation was a result of clay content, length of baking, and temperature in the kiln.[3]

Mizner was also producing light fixtures, andirons, and ornamental gates and grilles on a limited basis. With the completion of the Everglades Club, Singer's direct need for *Las Manos* ended. In 1919 Mizner bought the buildings and equipment from Singer, speculating that his own architectural commissions would cover the costs of production and that Mizner clay products, being first-rate, had a sales potential to other architects and individual clients. He commented, "There was no way of figuring out whether it was a winner or loser, as we were making something that could not be bought in the United States."[4]

The adventure was successful. By 1925 the firm had been considerably expanded with quarter-million dollar net profits. Mizner Industries, Incorporated was formed, buying out *Las Manos*, Addison Mizner Industries, and Antigua Shops, Inc. Mizner Industries, Incorporated advertised itself as "Manufacturers of pottery, roof and floor tile, period furniture, wicker, upholstering, repairing, antique millwork and hardware, bronze sash, wrought iron, stained and leaded glass windows, reconstructed and ornamental stone, and imitation marble."[5] A sales office was opened on Via Mizner and sales brochures were widely circulated.

The basic Mizner floor tile was unglazed. The firm recommended an oil wax treatment which would heighten the natural color of the terra cotta and create a soft patina (colorplate 1). Glazed tiles were produced in these solid colors: Mizner blue, light blue, Valencia blue, light green, neutral green, green, yellow, orange, red, brown, blue-black, and black. No patterned, multi-colored tiles were manufactured at Mizner Industries. The tiles came in six basic shapes: diamond, octagon, rectangle, picket (double-ended), hexagon, and triangle and these shapes came in various sizes and dissections. The result was an almost infinite variety of floor patterns and in its brochure the firm illustrated sixteen combinations and indicated by catalogue number which tiles should be purchased.

Mizner's name was associated nationwide with two colors which he had popularized; Mizner blue, a turquoise, and Mizner yellow, a soft lemon. The colors were in vogue for everything. Discussing the latest fashions for hats, the *Palm Beach Daily News* reported:

Next to white in favor for millinery as well as other wearing apparel is the 'Mizner yellow'. It is a shade between the mimosa and the apricot and has found favor because of its almost universal becomingness. Although all shades of yellow from the pale canary to the deep tangerine are sought in millinery, none of them has created the furor of the 'Mizner shade'.[6]

Another important product of Mizner Industries was ornamental pottery. The pots were produced in plain clay or in solid glazes. The styles were numerous, but all were designed "to follow as nearly as possible the original productions of Old Spain."[7] Most popular was the "Ali Baba" which

came in at least two sizes; one which would have provided ample hiding space for a man. Most jars were named after cities in Spain, but the styles were so generically Hispanic that naming was merely a convenience for the client.

The Mizner Industries publications all suggested that pottery could be effectively used to integrate an indoor and outdoor color scheme. In his architectural design, Mizner sought to break down the concept of interior vs. exterior spaces by creating open loggia rooms, glazed cloisterways, wide balconies, and patios. The pottery served as a color means to achieve this same goal. The larger pots were designed for small trees and the smaller pots which came with saucers "to enable you to bring your favorite plant or flower indoors". It was also noted, "...harmonizing shades of Mizner pots and bowls brighten those parts of the garden which are not in bloom".[18]

Stonework also came to be an important division of Mizner Industries. Quarry key stone, brain coral, was brought via railroad from a Mizner-owned quarry on Islamorada in the Florida Keys. Quarry stone was used principally for outdoor terraces and stairs, but Mizner used it in a rough cut form as the foundation for the Paul Moore house.

Artificial or cast stone was developed by Mizner and Mizner Industries to decrease building construction time and to keep down costs. The publicity division wrote:

In olden days when people had more time and labor was less expensive, the use of stone was not prohibitive. Stones could be shipped long distances. With the increase in building and increased costs, less and less of the real stone was available. Then came the use of artificial stone. The first productions of this kind were somewhat elementary. We had the grey, or white, commonly known to most of us, and not much different from our cement sidewalks. Such was the infancy of artificial stone.

What a change you will see upon your visit to the factory of

Mizner Industries. Gorgeous colors have been introduced. Travertine, marble, stones of every description have been imitated, and new types created....The experimental department is going on to still greater accomplishments, bringing out new things all the time.[9]

Immediately it must have become apparent to Mizner that even if his clients could afford to pay the charges for authentic Medieval and Renaissance doorways, columns, and windows, there was not a sufficient number available for import from Europe and Latin America. Shipping was slow. Reconstruction was difficult. Since native Florida stone was scarce, the experimentation with poured stone was undertaken. Although the specific contents remain undefined, the material poured was a mixture of coquina shell, lime, and a cement compound. Mizner Industries designed its own pieces and it copied examples from Spain. Moulds were made and poured at the factory. The pitting and slightly brown coloring in cast or poured stone is a result of voids made by gases escaping from bicarbonate of soda, another ingredient of the final casting compound. Chips, cracks, and breaks in the authentic pieces came out identically in the finished products. Soon even original production moulds were made with realistic mars and fractures. Workmen, under Mizner's instruction, did intentional damage to their finished products in order to make the pieces look antique. One stoneworker whose story is typical related:

I got so mad once when Mr. Mizner came along. He said the job was good. 'Do you have a hatchet?' I thought that he was kidding me, so I went and got a hatchet. He knocked corners off my pieces here and there. Then he told me to patch them on again but so that the patches were noticeable from 25 feet away. I couldn't believe it.[10]

The production of the stonework division was extensive in diversity and in quantity of products. Available to the interested buyer were all items imaginable from small medallions to sixteen-foot cloister windows. There were columns, capitals, crests, fireplaces, fountains, doorways *ad infinitum*. One of the major difficulties in identifying Mizner buildings is the presence of Mizner Industries stonework on non-Mizner buildings. All local builders and architects purchased from the factory.

Mizner Industries' brochures were quick to stress that many buildings, even non-Spanish ones, used the stonework products, citing the Gulf Stream Title and Mortgage Co. in West Palm Beach and St. Edward's Church in Palm Beach. Prices were included to aid the prospective buyer. For example:

Gothic windows — $168.50 per one opening complete. Each additional opening $113.50.

No. 5007 — wall fountain, height 63″, width 25½″, projection of bowl 15″, height of pedestal 36″. Price $40.25. Can be supplied without pedestal, No. 5007-A. Price $12.00.[11]

And two last notes indicate the extensiveness of the sales:

The designs illustrated in this folder are only a small part of our full line. Send in your plans or sketches for estimates. All prices include crating and hauling, F.O.B., West Palm Beach, Florida.[12]

The market was intended to be a broad one.

Another operation of the stonework division involved the production of "precast plastering", highly-ornate plaster coffered ceilings and mouldings. These were also available commercially. One advertisement commended the work of Mizner Industries at the First Church of Christ Scientist in Orlando, Florida; "One of many excellent precast and run plaster contracts we have completed with high praise from the owners. Screen work as shown costs about $3.00 per sq.

MIZNER INDUSTRIES INCORPORATED

MANUFACTURERS OF

POTTERY · ROOF & FLOOR TILE · PERIOD FURNITURE · WICKER · UPHOLSTERING · REPAIRING
ANTIQUE MILLWORK AND HARDWARE · BRONZE SASH · WROUGHT IRON
STAINED AND LEADED GLASS WINDOWS · RECONSTRUCTED AND
ORNAMENTAL STONE · IMITATION MARBLE

Factories:
PENN ROAD
WEST PALM BEACH
FLORIDA

Telephones:
OFFICE 2-1193
FACTORY 7117
SHOW ROOMS 2-1193

337 Worth Avenue
P. O. Box 2068
PALM BEACH, FLORIDA

No. 2042

No. 1136

No. 2041

No. 1183

No. 2043

Saragoza

Avilla

No. 2044

No. 2040

Granada

Jerez

No. 717

No. 2034

MATCHLESS QUALITY MIZNER PRODUCTS

There are products that only Mizner Industries can offer.

Unusual tile and pottery.

Perfectly reproduced period furniture.

Artistic stone.

Extraordinary wrought iron.

Beautiful leaded and stained glass.

Simple or elaborate ceilings.

Complete paneled rooms.

Durable bronze sash.

And many other exceptional products.

No. 1185

Cordova

No. 2036

Andalucia

No. 2034

No. 2037

Mizner Industries Sale's Brochure, ca. 1924.

ft. Send plans for complete estimates".[13]

Ornamental ironwork comprised yet another division of Mizner Industries. The products included grilles, gates, lanterns, candelabra, outdoor furniture, planters, andirons, and even lightswitches. Many ironwork products were copies of authentic Spanish antiques. A sixteenth century gate could be purchased from an impoverished Spanish *don*, shipped across the Atlantic and painstakingly copied at the Mizner factories. Variations on the originals were simple. But a lightswitch was not a part of sixteenth century Spain. There was no example to copy. And yet, Mizner, in keeping with his architectural philosophy, would not have tolerated the ordinary Sears and Roebuck lightplate. Mizner Industries designed a wrought iron plate which was an enlarged version, approximately 7" x 7", of the metal studs which bound together the heavy boards of the wooden doors of Old Spain. The switch replaced the central tie-bolt. It was a traditional, decorative, and functional response to a modern problem.

The craftsmanship of the wrought iron was exceedingly fine. The metal shop included machine tools, but much of the finishing was by hand. In a grille, for example, soldering was avoided and banding, the traditional method of linking parts together, was used. The latter is much more difficult and time-consuming, but the end product is much finer structurally and aesthetically. It was the small touches which assured the superior quality of Mizner products.

An aging process was used on the ironwork products because Mizner disliked the highly-polished, black surface of new wrought iron. A workman described one such process, "At Mizner's we let the ornamental wrought iron rust. We dipped lamps or whatever in an acid solution and overnight they would rust. Then, we'd rinse them off and put regular floor wax on them and then rub them with 'rotten stone'."[14]

An important side industry was the production of leaded and stained glass. Leaded glass was used extensively on Mizner buildings for the architect liked the mellow light such windows yielded. In describing an event at his Via Mizner apartment, Mizner wrote:

One year I had every afternoon for two weeks, from six to seven o'clock, the New York String Quartet. They sat in the middle of the great Gothic room, with the lights on their music stands as the only illumination, and played divinely, as daylight died through the soft tints of the colored glass. People came in quietly, without greetings, and sank into big chairs, and one felt medieval as the footman stole about lighting great cathedral candles here and there.[15]

The preferred colors for leaded glass windows were blue, amber, and amethyst. Stained glass was done on commission for churches, but again the presence of such a window in no way indicates that the building is a Mizner design.

A second offshoot industry involved the production of bronze sliding sashes. With the architect's extensive use of heavily-fenestrated rooms or cloisterways in his buildings, it became imperative for aesthetic and for functional reasons to employ a new window framing system. Wood and metal frames available rotted out from the ocean spray and they were visually bulky, detracting from the open-air effect Mizner was seeking to achieve. Mizner designed a sophisticated bronze window and door frame which was thin, weather resistant, and operable. Doors and windows were fitted into the frames which were designed to slide by overlapping another frame or to disappear into the wall or floor structure when open.

Furniture is the most familiar product of Mizner Industries. That division, which was officially opened in 1923, advertised:

In a distinctly modern world we have a factory making 'antique' furniture. For example: given one half of a door of the

Because of the great variety, is is impossible to show all of the products of the Mizner Industries in a catalog. We have made a few selections which are shown below. If you fail to find what you want, Mizner Industries can make it, if it is not already on hand.

No. 1186

No. 1189

No. 1180

No. 2039

No. 1182

No. 2035

No. 1181

No. 1146

No. 1145

No. 1158

No. 1158-A

No. 1163

No. 1086

No. 1115

No. 1187

No. 1125

No. 1162

No. 1011

No. 1184

No. 1174

No. 1177

No. 1152

No. 1170

No. 1169

No. 1188

If you desire any further information about any article, shown, please mention stock number.

Mizner Industries Sales Brochure, ca. 1924.

Sixteenth Century, the Mizner Industries will make the other half with age, worm holes, and all the scars of time. If you have a Seventeenth Century chair and need two, take it to the factory. They will faithfully reproduce it. It is claimed by visitors that it is practically impossible to pick the original from the reproductions.[16]

A Mizner cabinetmaker described the working process: "He [Mizner] imported from Spain and then copied. He also used photographs. He might change a piece some, but he was really after a resemblance to the original."[17] Mizner's scrapbooks frequently contain sketched details of chair legs or bed backs pasted next to photographs or clippings of an original Spanish example. Mizner's working process is clearly indicated.

Beds, tables, taborets, chests, dressing tables, stools, all pieces of furniture imaginable were manufactured. Mizner reproduced Spanish sixteenth and seventeenth century furniture. He appears to have stayed away from unique examples, preferring to recreate fine, but typical pieces. Most popular was the traditional plank or trestle table with wrought iron supports. The finest walnut was used and prices were high: "No. 1051 — Height 33", Width 32", Length 5'6", Price, $250".[18] Two degrees of quality were produced: a superior, handcrafted line for the private residences of Mizner's wealthy clients and a good, sturdy line with little or no hand attention for the hotel rooms in Boca Raton, for the Embassy Club, and for similar places where public use demanded a large repetitive quantity which would receive hard and varied use. The superior quality pieces are extremely difficult to distinguish from authentic Spanish antiques.

Antiquing was an important part of the furniture finishing process. Worm holes, chips, scratches, splits, all are a part of antique furniture and without such instant aging Mizner's furniture would have been merely contemporary reproductions. A craftsman described the intricate process for making wormholes:

First you take an icepick and push it into the soft part of the raw wood. The soft part is the area nearest the bark and this is also a good part to take advantage of for splitting and chipping. You put the icepick or file into the wood, wrap a rag around the handle, and hit it. This forces the point deep and the hole stays. When you put finish on the wood, the hole closes up and it looks authentic.[19]

Mizner solved a difficult problem for the living room by creating his own unique sofa and armchair. Early Spanish furniture offered no prototypes for these pieces, and yet the 1920's client naturally expected these comfortable conveniences in his home. Thus was born a squat upholstered armchair which affectionately was dubbed a "Papa Mizner" or "Mizner Senior". It was a chair made for a large heavy man for it was low, broad, sturdy, spacious, and straight-backed with firm, padded, wide arms. The catalogue description read: "No. 1011 — Height, 41", Seat, 38" x 43" as shown, Price $350".[20] A "junior" version of the chair was also offered. The chairs usually were covered in velvet with contrasting satin banding or fringe or in flocked velvet with fringe. A Mizner Industries advertisement rendered the chair the following justice, ". . . the Mizner chair, a distinctive product; a deep, soft, upholstered chair you will never forget. Sitting in one is like resting in a fleecy cloud".[21]

The sofa with arms was an expanded version of the armchair, although the seat was narrower and the upholstery less deep. The sofa was based on the traditional straight-backed Spanish bench. It was cumbersome, less than comfortable, but majestic and sympathetic with its Spanish neighbors.

Wicker, or more correctly, rattan furniture for outdoor use was also produced. The designs for rattan pieces were far more progressive than for any other Mizner decorative arts products. Available were chairs, two-seater settees, and chaise lounges. All were straight-backed and most models had wide, flat arms. The lounge chair did not recline and its footrest was permanently fixed. It appears that the rattan was unpainted, perhaps preserved with a mat varnish. Prices were quite reasonable with an armchair available at $15.75. For outdoor use a wrought iron chair, chaise lounge, and tables with benches were also manufactured.[22]

After 1924 Mizner Industries began producing doors and room paneling in "woodite", a composite material of wood and a cohesive compound which could be poured and cast. Woodite could be painted, stained, nailed, and sawn like regular wood. The woodite process was patented and Mizner Industries was seeking ways to make production even more economical. Woodite reproductions made from moulds taken from original Spanish doors and dados were reasonably cheap, in comparison to the original, authentic in details, highly-believable in appearance, and moreover permitted the paneling of a complete room without an extensive search in Europe for a room suitable for reinstallation.[23]

Mizner Industries remained solvent after the 1926 land crash and still prospered after the two hurricanes. It was financially a significant help to Mizner when he was struggling to recoup his losses. The plant was sold from Mizner's estate and continued to operate until the mid-1950's as Mizner Industries.

ⴰⴰ Mizner Industries Notes

1 Addison Mizner, Incomplete Manuscript, ca. 1932, Private Collection, p. 55.

2 Ida M. Tarbell, *Florida Architecture of Addison Mizner*, William Helburn, Inc., New York City, 1928, n.p.

3 Interview with José Diaz, West Palm Beach, Fla., November, 1976 and "The Handmade Potteries of Paris Singer Most Unique", *Palm Beach Weekly News*, December 13, 1918, pp. 1, 6.

4 *Mizner Incomplete Manuscript*, p. 55.

5 Advertising Brochure for Mizner Industries, Inc. (general), n.p., Palm Beach, Fla., ca. 1924, n.p. (Collection of the Historical Society of Palm Beach County).

6 *Palm Beach Daily News*, January 8, 1925, p. 3.

7 Advertising Brochure for Mizner Industries, Inc. (pottery), n.p., Palm Beach, Fla., ca. 1924, n.p. (Collection of the Historical Society of Palm Beach County).

8 *Ibid.*

9 Don Morris, "Mizner Industries: Details of the Palm Beaches' Greatest Manufactory" in *The New Palm Beaches of 1929*, n.p., West Palm Beach, Fla., 1929, p. 2 of article.

10 Interview with Joe Mueller, West Palm Beach, Fla., February, 1975.

11 Advertising Brochure for Mizner Industries, Inc. (stonework), n.p., Palm Beach, Fla., ca. 1924, n.p. (Collection of the Historical Society of Palm Beach County).

12 *Ibid.*

13 *Ibid.*

14 Interview with F. L. Schindler, West Palm Beach, Fla., March, 1976.

15 *Mizner Incomplete Manuscript*, p. 121.

16 *The New Palm Beaches of 1929*, p. 2 of article. Mizner required that he be consulted about the furnishings of at least the first floor of his buildings. He wrote, "...I was adamant about having things in keeping". *Mizner Incomplete Manuscript*, p. 75.

17 *Interview with F. L. Schindler.*

18 *Mizner Industries' Brochure (general).*

19 *Interview with F. L. Schindler.*

20 *Mizner Industries' Brochure (general).*

21 *The New Palm Beaches of 1929*, p. 2 of article.

22 *Mizner Industries' Brochure (general).*

23 Don Morris, "Woodite, Incorporated: The Palm Beaches' Newest Industry" in *The New Palm Beaches of 1929*, n.p., West Palm Beach, Fla., 1929, p. 1 of article.

Addison Mizner Buildings and Projects

Identification of all residents is by the name of the original owner

Description	Designed	B—Built P—Project U—Uncertain	Destroyed	Seriously Altered
Alterations to the Hotel Rand, 142 W. 49th St., N.Y.C.	1907	B		X
Alterations and additions to the Old Cow Bay Manor House, Port Washington, L.I.	1910	B	?	
Completion of Town House for Mrs. Stephen Brown, 154 E. 70th St., N.Y.C.	1912	B		X
Residence for Mrs. William A. Prime, Roslyn, L.I.	ca. 1912	B	?	
Residence for Mr. and Mrs. John Alley Parker, Sands Point, L.I.	1912	B	?	
Residence for Raymond Hitchcock, Great Neck, L.I.	1914	B	?	
Residence for Bourke Cochran, Sands Point, L.I.	1914	B	?	
Chinese Tea House for Mrs. O. H. P. Belmont, Great Neck, L.I.	1914	B	?	
"White Pine Camp" for Archibald White, Adirondack Mountains	1914	B	?	
Beach House for Mrs. O. H. P. Belmont, Great Neck, L.I.	1915	U		
Residence for I. Townsend Burden, Greenvale, L.I.	1916	U		
Residence for Mrs. Stephen Brown, Piping Rock, L.I.	1917	U		
The Everglades Club, Worth Ave., Palm Beach, Fla. Alterations 1919-1926 by Mizner	1918	B		X
Maisonette Buildings, Everglades Club, Worth Ave., Palm Beach, Fla.	1918-1926	B	X	
"El Mirasol," Residence for Mr. and Mrs. Edward Stotesbury, N. County Rd., Palm Beach, Fla.	1919	B	X	
"El Salano," Residence for Mr. Harold Vanderbilt (originally occupied by Addison Mizner), 720 S. Ocean Blvd., Palm Beach, Fla.	1919	B	X	
"Amado," Residence for Charles Munn, 455 N. County Rd., Palm Beach, Fla.	1919	B		
"Louwana," Residence for Gurnee Munn, 473 N. County Rd., Palm Beach, Fla.	1919	B		
"La Bellucia," Residence for W. L. Kingsley, 1200 S. Ocean Blvd., Palm Beach, Fla.	1920	B		
Residence for H. C. Clark, Palm Beach, Fla.	1920	P		
"Villa Flora," Residence for Edward Shearson, 110 Dunbar Rd., Palm Beach, Fla.	1920	B		
"Casa de Leoni," Residence for Leonard Thomas, 450 Worth Ave., Palm Beach, Fla.	1920	B		
"Casa Bendita," Residence for John S. Phipps, N. County Rd., Palm Beach, Fla.	1921+	B	X	
"Concha Marina," Residence for George Sloan, 102 Jungle Rd., Palm Beach, Fla.	1921	B		
Residence for W. S. Kilmer, Palm Beach, Fla.	1922	U		
"Casa Maria Marrone," Residence for Barclay Warburton, 480 Worth Ave., Palm Beach, Fla.	1922	B		X
Residence for Joseph Cudahy, 135 Grace Trail, Palm Beach, Fla.	1922	B		
"Sin Cuidado," Residence for Edward S. Moore, 1800 S. Ocean Blvd., Palm Beach, Fla.	1922 (1924-1926)	B		
Residence for Mr. and Mrs. William Gray Warden, 112 Seminole Rd., Palm Beach, Fla.	1922	B		
Residence for Mme Jenette Gais (Mrs. O. F. Woodward), just South of Barton on Ocean Blvd., (unlocated) Palm Beach, Fla.	1922	B		
"Villa Tranquilla," Residence for DeGrimm Renfro, El Vedado and Ocean Blvd., Palm Beach, Fla.	1923	B	X	
Residence for Mr. and Mrs. George L. Mesker, Royal Palm Way, Palm Beach, Fla.	1923	B	X	

Description	Designed	B—Built P—Project U—Uncertain	Destroyed	Seriously Altered
Residence for Dr. Preston P. Satterwhite, Ocean Blvd., Palm Beach, Fla.	1923	B	X	
Residence for D. H. Carstairs, Esq., 280 N. Ocean Blvd., Palm Beach, Fla.	1923	B		
Residence for Joseph Speidel, Palm Beach, Fla. (unlocated)	1923	B		
Store Building for H. Bendel, Esq., Seminole Ave., Palm Beach, Fla.	1923	P		
Residence for Angier Duke, Esq. Palm Beach, Fla.	1923	P		
Residence for Arthur B. Claflin, 800 S. County Rd., Palm Beach, Fla.	1923	B		
"Playa Riente," Residence for Joshua S. Cosden, N. Ocean Blvd., Palm Beach, Fla.	1923+	B	X	
"The Towers," Residence for William Woods, N. County Rd., Palm Beach, Fla.	1923+	B	X	
Gulf Stream Club, Gulf Stream, Fla.	1923	B		X
Residence for Wilson Mizner, 237 Worth Ave., Palm Beach, Fla.	ca. 1924	B		X
Via Mizner and Villa Mizner, off Worth Ave., Palm Beach, Fla.	1924	B		
Singer Building, Royal Palm Way, Palm Beach, Fla.	ca. 1924	B	X	
Residence for Ysabel Chase, 17-Mile Dr., Pebble Beach, Calif.	1924	B		
Residence for Mr. and Mrs. Nat Spingold, 152 Wells Rd., Palm Beach, Fla.	ca. 1924	B		
Residence of John F. Harris, 4 El Bravo Way, Palm Beach, Fla. (partially Marion Wyeth)	ca. 1924	B		
Residence of the Honorable C. T. Wynn, Palm Beach, Fla. (unlocated)	ca. 1924	B		

Description	Designed	B—Built P—Project U—Uncertain	Destroyed	Seriously Altered
"Lagomar," Residence of John Magee, 1560 S. Ocean Blvd., Palm Beach, Fla.	ca. 1924	B		X
"Casa Nana," Residence for George Rasmussen, 780 S. Ocean Blvd., Palm Beach, Fla.	ca. 1924	B		
"Collado Hueco," Residence for Paul Moore, 1820 S. Ocean Blvd., Palm Beach, Fla.	ca. 1924	B		
"La Guerida," Residence for Rodman Wanamaker, 1113 N. Ocean Blvd., Palm Beach, Fla.	ca. 1924	B		
"El Sarimento," Residence for Anthony J. Drexel Biddle, Esq., 150 S. Ocean Blvd., Palm Beach, Fla.	1924	B		
Seaboard Railroad Station (no location)	1924	P		
The Plaza Shops, 240-246 N. County Rd., Palm Beach, Fla.	1924	B		
Residence for Mrs. William K. Vanderbilt, Palm Beach, Fla.	1925	P		
Boynton Town Hall, Boynton, Fla.	1925	U		
Woman's Club, Boynton, Fla.	1925	B		
Ritz-Carlton Cloister Hotel, Boca Raton, Fla.	1925	B		X
Administration Building, Boca Raton, Fla.	1925	B		
Hotel Garage, Boca Raton, Fla.	1925	B	X	
Town Hall, Boca Raton, Fla. (not completed by firm)	1925	B		
"Floresta," Housing Development Boca Raton, Fla. (29 houses)	1925	B		
Residence for Mr. and Mrs. Halpine Smith, 325 Chilean Ave., Palm Beach, Fla.	1925	B		
Via Parigi, off Worth Ave., Palm Beach, Fla.	1925	B		X
Bridge for Boca Raton Inlet, Boca Raton, Fla.	1925	P		

Description	Designed	B—Built P—Project U—Uncertain	Destroyed	Seriously Altered
Housing Development (Hotel/apartment complex), Boca Raton, Fla.	1925	P		
Residence for Anderson T. Herd, Esq., Boca Raton, Fla.	ca. 1925	P		
Residence for Countess Bai-Lihmé, Palm Beach or Boca Raton, Fla.	1925	P		
E. B. Davis Office Building, Boca Raton, Fla.	1925	P		
Las Carreras Jockey Club, Boca Raton, Fla.	1926	P		
Apartment Building for W. H. Dunagan, Esq., Boca Raton, Fla.	1926	P		
Residence for Dr. Maurice Druker, Boca Raton, Fla.	1926	P		
Small Development Houses for Dr. Maurice Druker, Boca Raton, Fla.	1926	P		
Whelan Villa, Boca Raton, Fla.	1926	P		
Residence for Mme Frances Alda, Boca Raton, Fla.	1926	P		
Residence for Mrs. H. Marshall Taylor, Jacksonville, Fla.	1926	U		
Riverside Baptist Church, King and Park Sts., Jacksonville, Fla.	1926	B		
Blue Heron Hotel, Singer Island (partially completed)	1926	B	X	
Boat House for Alice DeLamar, Palm Beach, Fla.	1926	P		
Bradley Ranch, Colorado Springs, Colorado	1927	U		
Renovation for Mrs. Glen Hodges, 306-312 Worth Ave., Palm Beach, Fla.	1927	B		X
Residence for Mr. and Mrs. J. D. Gedney, 1720 S. Ocean Blvd., Manalapan, Fla.	1928	B		
Beauville Beach Club, Windsor, Canada	ca. 1928	P		
Residence for Dan Murphy, Los Angeles, Calif.	ca. 1928	U		
Nurses' Lodge, Good Samaritan Hospital, West Palm Beach, Fla.	1928	B(?)	X	
Embassy Club, Royal Palm Way, Palm Beach, Fla., (now Society of the Four Arts)	1928	B		X
Sea Island Club, Sea Island, Ga.	1928	B		X
Office Building for Harris, Winthrop & Co., Miami, Fla.	1928	P		
Residence for John F. Harris, Miami Beach, Fla.	1928	P		
Residence for Percival Foerderer, Bryn Mawr, Pa.	1928-29	B		
Memorial Fountain, County Rd., Palm Beach, Fla.	1929	B		
Fox Chapel Country Club, Pittsburgh, Pa.	1929	P		
Residence for Mr. and Mrs. A. E. Dietrich, Monteceito, (Santa Barbara), Calif.	1929-30	B		
E. F. Hutton Brokerage Co., 264 N. County Rd., Palm Beach, Fla.	1930	B		
Residence for Hugh Dillman, Grosse Point, Mich.	1930	P		
Residence for Mr. and Mrs. Alex Camp, Dallas, Texas	1930	U		
Palm Beach Post Office, Palm Beach, Fla.	1931	P		
Residence for Mr. and Mrs. F. C. Williams, 510 Park St. North, St. Petersburg, Fla.	1931	B		
Bonsack Shopping Complex, Miami Beach, Fla.	ca. 1931	P		
Residence for W. F. Bonsack, Miami Beach, Fla.	1931	P		
Residence for Mr. and Mrs. K. D. Alexander, Boca Raton and Palm Beach, Fla.	1925 (1932)	P		
Hotel and Theatre Building, Belle Glade, Fla.	1932	P		

▲▲ Selected Bibliography

Primary Sources

The Mizner design scrapbooks and the architect's complete library are available for consultation by scholars at the Society of the Four Arts Library in Palm Beach, Florida. A large number of architectural drawings from the Mizner firm are in the collections of The Historical Society of Palm Beach County and in the possession of Mr. Mack Ritchie. The Mizner family still own sketchbooks, photoalbums, and some letters. Much of that material is on loan to The Oakland Museum, Oakland, California.

Mizner, Addison. *Cynic's Calendar of Revised Wisdom*, n. p., San Francisco, 1903-1909.

Mizner, Addison. *Cynic's Calendar Revived*, n. p., San Francisco, 1917.

Mizner, Addison. *The Lark*, Willis Polk et al., San Francisco, 1895-1897.

Mizner, Addison. *The Many Mizners*, Sears Publishing Co., New York City, 1932. (Mizner's autobiography, written by the architect himself, covers his life to 1915.)

Mizner, Addison. Untitled, Incomplete Manuscript, ca. 1932, Private Collection. (The second half of the architect's autobiography is incomplete and stops abruptly in 1925.)

Secondary Sources

"Bungalows in the Spanish Manner Adapted to Meet American Ideals", *The Ladies' Home Journal*, February, 1927, p. 36.

"The Florida House", an interview of Addison Mizner by John Taylor Boyd in *Arts and Decoration*, Vol. 32, January, 1930, pp. 36-40+.

Johnson, Alva. *The Legendary Mizners*, Farrar, Straus, and Young, New York City, 1942 (1950, 1952, 1953). (A relatively accurate book written in entertaining journalistic language.)

Johnson, Alva. Profile on Addison Mizner, *New Yorker*, Vol. 28, November 22, 29, December 6, 13, 1952. (A highly-readable article which rehashes the above book. Inaccuracies exist.)

"The Old Cow Bay Manor House", *Architectural Record*, March, 1917, n.p.

"A Spanish House in Monterey", *Architect and Engineer*, Vol. 80, February, 1925, pp. 50-51, 92-95.

Tarbell, Ida M. *Florida Architecture of Addison Mizner*, William Helburn, Inc., New York City, 1928. (A good 1920's discussion of Mizner and his work; quite accurate.)

The *Palm Beach Daily News*, *Palm Beach Life*, and the *Palm Beach Weekly News* of the 1920's also provide much information on Mizner and his architecture. Advertising brochures for Mizner Industries, available at The Historical Society of Palm Beach County, provide the greatest information on Mizner's decorative arts.

⋀⋀ List of Lenders and Participants

Anonymous

Mr. Draper Babcock

Beinecke Rare Book and Manuscript Library, Yale University

Boca Raton Cloisters, Mr. and Mrs. L. Bert Stephens

Dr. C. Earl Cooper, Pastor, Riverside Baptist Church,
    Jacksonville

Commander and Mrs. Harold L. Crossman

Mrs. Ray B. Dame

Mrs. Woolworth Donahue

Justice E. Harris Drew

Honorable and Mrs. Guildford Dudley

The Everglades Club

Mr. and Mrs. Lester W. Geisler

Gulf Stream Golf Club

Mr. and Mrs. Rodman A. Heeren

The Henry Morrison Flagler Museum

Mr. and Mrs. A. Lee Hicks

The Historical Society of Palm Beach County

Mr. and Mrs. Kim Mizner Hollins

Mrs. John C. Jessup

Mrs. Valerie Ellis Johnson

The Ladies' Home Journal

Mrs. Alice Mizner Lewitin

Mr. and Mrs. Enrique Mendoza

Norton Gallery of Art

The Oakland Museum, Oakland, California

Mr. and Mrs. Herman Reich

Mr. Karl Riddle and Mrs. Mavorette Riddle Hart

Mr. Mack Ritchie

Mr. and Mrs. Mortimer Sachs

Mr. Mike Slate

Mrs. Halpine Smith

Society of the Four Arts

Col. A. C. Tisdelle

Mr. and Mrs. Kyril Vassilev

PRINTED IN U.S.A.   SOUTHEASTERN PRINTING COMPANY, INC., STUART, FLORIDA